Advance Praise for *Choosing the Hero*

"A wonderful book about the extraordinary camaraderie between Africa's first woman president Ellen Johnson Sirleaf and her loyal friend and political ally, Riva Levinson . . . a must-read for all those interested in ... Liberia's recent and turbulent history, and the immense power of friendship and loyalty."

—JOHNNIE CARSON, FORMER U.S. ASSISTANT SECRETARY OF STATE FOR AFRICAN AFFAIRS

"A deeply moving story of two extraordinary women, from very different backgrounds, who worked together through thick and thin and achieved so much ... I would highly recommend this book to all."

—JOYCE BANDA, FORMER PRESIDENT OF MALAWI

"A riveting and compelling story that restores one's faith in humanity ... a profound lesson to all of us on the vital importance of courage and perseverance to the pursuit of a life of purpose."

—TONY ELUMELU, CHAIRMAN OF HEIRS HOLDINGS, NIGERIA

"A deeply personal and thoughtful book on some of the most important foreign policy issues of our time and a great read!"

—LLOYD PIERSON, FORMER DIRECTOR, U.S. PEACE CORPS, FORMER PRESIDENT, AFRICAN DEVELOPMENT FOUNDATION

"A compelling set of stories ... about how political capital was built by addition, multiplication, patience, and strategy by Ellen Johnson Sirleaf and Riva Levinson.

—WILLIAM R. SWEENEY JR., PRESIDENT AND CEO, INTERNATIONAL FOUNDATION FOR ELECTORAL SYSTEMS

"Peace and democracy seemed far, far off to Liberians when brutal warlord Charles Taylor ruled. This fast-paced, crisply told story of Liberia's rebirth under Ellen Johnson Sirleaf is inspiring and impressively honest."

    —U.S. Representative Ed Royce

"Riva Levinson gives us a peek behind the curtain of how American foreign policy is formulated and practiced. A thoroughly engaging read from cover to cover."

    —U.S. Senator Jeff Flake

"The inspiring story of two brilliant women who overcame the odds to make positive change in Liberia. A must-read for any aspiring global change maker!"

    —Dr. Rajesh Panjabi, CEO, Last Mile Health, *TIME's* 100 Most Influential People 2016

"A book that reads like Le Carré, if Le Carré was a combination of killer politico and Tina Fey ... smart, heartbreaking, funny, inspiring, and an unbelievably entertaining read."

    —Dan Gordon, screenwriter of The Hurricane

"Riva's story reminds us that often the best, most challenging work comes to us when we least expect it and most need it. Her connection with President Sirleaf helped Liberia turn an important page in its history."

    —U.S. Senator Chris Coons

CHOOSING THE HERO

CHOOSING THE HERO

My Improbable Journey and the Rise of Africa's
First Woman President

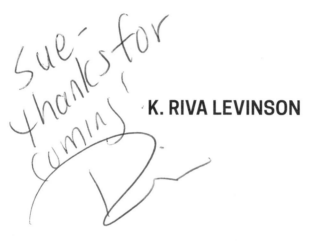

K. RIVA LEVINSON

Kiwai
media

WASHINGTON, D.C   LAGOS   PARIS   LONDON

CHOOSING THE HERO
My Improbable Journey and the Rise of Africa's First Woman President
By K. Riva Levinson

For all inquiries, address Publisher's Office, Kiwai Media, Inc.,12 Timber Creek Lane, Newark, DE 19711 USA. Tel: +1 (855) 707 2747. Publisher: David Applefield, info@kiwaimedia.com

Interior design by Stephan Cuber (Bern, Switzerland), www.diaphan.ch.
Cover design by Faceout Studio, Jeff Miller, www.faceoutstudio.com.
Proofreading by Mayanne Wright (mayanne@aol.com).
Kiwai Media Online and digital marketing and social media by Ingenium Media, Monaco.

Published by Kiwai Media, Inc.

10 9 8 7 6 5 4 3 2 1
Library of Congress Cataloging-in-Publication Data is available.

ISBN   978-1-937247-03-4 (print)
ISBN   978-1-937247-04-1 (ebook)
Kiwai Media, First Edition: June 2016, signed and numbered 1–100.

www.kiwaimedia.com

CONTENTS

(top) Oma (middle left) with her husband Jacques Kroner, Riva's mother Edith, Aunt Ellie, at their Berlin home, Spring 1936.

(bottom) Oma with Riva, Riva's mother, Aunt Ellie, sister Kim, brother Kevan, and friends, December 1985, Long Island, NY.

DEDICATION

In loving memory of my grandmother, my Oma,
Manja Pakter Kroner, and to my parents,
Milton Maurice Levinson and Edith Kroner Levinson.

FOREWORD

By Ellen Johnson Sirleaf
President of the Republic of Liberia
Nobel Laureate

I would not have selected the title *Choosing the Hero* for Riva's book. I might have settled on something such as *The Advocate* or *The Secret Weapon*. Because that is how I see Riva, through the prism of my own struggle: a fierce fighter for me and for the Liberian people, a partner and friend now for nearly two decades. What I did not come to realize until I read Riva's book was how I fit into her life and into her own search for meaning. It is not often that someone surprises me.

I met Riva twenty years ago in 1997 when I was looking for someone to support me in Washington, DC, as I was planning my return from exile to run for the presidency of Liberia against Charles Taylor, then a warlord, now a convicted war criminal. While Riva came highly recommended to me, I had doubts. I thought it important for the person supporting me in Washington to have US government credentials, to be more of an *insider*. But after meeting Riva, I came to think otherwise. I saw a flexibility of thought and an ability to maneuver and persuade that I thought would be important. When I think back to that first interview over coffee, as Riva slyly tried to hide her pregnancy, what I saw was a fighter. And that was exactly what I needed.

As this book reveals, Riva worked with me on my first presidential campaign in 1997; through the regional civil war that unfolded after Taylor's victory; during my exile in Côte d'Ivoire and the two years of the transitional government after peace was negotiated with Liberia's warring factions; and then, on my presidential campaign in 2005 when at last I emerged victorious. During nearly all of that time, Riva's tireless efforts were provided pro-bono. Of all my friends and staff, my constituents and supporters in Liberia and around the world, even my own family, few believed in me like Riva did.

I remember Riva trying to convince a skeptical Congress, Administration and State Department in Washington that a woman could emerge as president of an African country. I recall her trip to Liberia with Amara Konneh, now my Finance Minister, advocating for public opinion polling in a country where opinions had never been properly assessed. I remember how in March 2006 Riva helped facilitate my first trip to Washington, DC, where I had the privilege as an elected head of state to deliver a speech to a Joint Meeting of Congress, a speech that Riva helped to prepare and that a young senator from Illinois, Barack Obama, said was one of the best he had ever heard delivered before the Chamber.

Riva's story could have ended at that moment, March 16, 2006. But Riva has gone on to provide invaluable advocacy for over another decade, working with four Liberian ambassadors to the US and successive US administrations, Democrat and Republican, to help consolidate peace in our country and support Liberia's emergence as a post-conflict success story.

Through Riva's words in this book, I am able to look back upon moments in my life, moments that I thought I owned solely, and see them afresh from a sympathetic but no less discerning eye. I am reminded that history could have shifted in a different direction numerous times, not only for me, but also for the people of my country. The seemingly disconnected moments in our lives—a singular conversation, an accidental encounter, an instinct, a hunch, a miscalculation, a powerful voice, a well-timed newspaper article—are in fact indispensable pieces of a puzzle that reveals itself over time. Riva captures so well the events that transformed the African continent. She was there, on the front lines. She reveals the crucial role that Washington played in Liberia's emergence from decades of armed conflict. And she presents some of the many unsung heroes in this story, including members of Congress and their key staff.

I encourage everyone to read this book. It tells my story from the special perspective of a woman who knows me well and was with me at every stage of the journey—a woman to whom I will always be grateful. But read this book also for the reason that it is as much Riva's story as it is mine.

—ELLEN JOHNSON SIRLEAF

(Photo: David Applefield)

Riva at Nobel Prize ceremony, Oslo, December 2011.

OSLO RÅDHUS

Pipervika, Oslo, Norway,
December 10, 2011

Oslo City Hall, *rådhus* in Norwegian, a simple, austere building exemplifying the functional Nordic trend in architecture of the 1930s, is perched on a hill across from the revered Nobel Institute in the heart of Pipervika, the government district of Oslo's small downtown. The red brick façade contrasts with the great hall it conceals. Magnificent in size and depth, the towering space resonates with grandeur and the echo of the carillon. The room is impeccably set for the royal affair that awaits, the 113-year tradition as dictated by the will of Alfred P. Nobel. The center front row is reserved for the Norwegian royal family, King Harald, Queen Sonja, Crown Prince Haakon and Crown Princess Mette-Marit. The stage is ready for the three Nobel Peace Laureates.

Rapt in awe, I am here as an invited guest to celebrate the 2011 prizes, awarded jointly this year to Ellen Johnson Sirleaf, the President of the Republic of Liberia, Leymah Gbowee also of Liberia, and Tawakkul Karman from Yemen. The three women have been cited "for their non-violent struggle for the safety of women and for women's rights to full participation in peace-building work."

It is extremely cold—minus eleven degrees Celsius. The security screening area is a virtual wind tunnel, as it proves impossible to keep the outside doors shut while moving a couple thousand people through the single entrance way. It is a good thing Ellen doesn't have to wait in line like the rest of us. She hates the cold and would never last out here.

My teeth are chattering and my ears aching thanks to my unwillingness to wear a hat that might flatten my hair. Vain decision, I admit to myself. I cup my ears with my thin, black velvet, elbow-length gloves, another useless wardrobe choice for this special day in frozen Oslo.

I take my seat in the second row on the right, flanking the Queen, and with an unobstructed view of the stage. Next to me is Jennie, Ellen's older sister, her best friend, and the rest of Ellen's close-knit family. It is a privileged seat and the most privileged place to be in the world on this Sunday, the tenth day of December, 2011.

Four trumpeters open the procession of the Nobel laureates. I spot Ellen leading the pack, followed by Leymah Gbowee and Tawakkul Kaman, each escorted by members of the Nobel Committee. The rich sound of the horns is powerful and I am overwhelmed with the magic of the moment. As I watch the three Nobel Laureates make their way down the red carpet, I think back to all that Ellen has been through since that summer day when we first met in her office at the United Nations, in July of 1996, during her exile from her native Liberia. My mind races through that struggle and revisits Ellen's decision to return home and challenge the rule of warlords. She failed not once, but twice.

I am reminded of the costs of those failures on her personally, and on her family. Ellen had to make many sacrifices as a young mother in Africa in the 1960s, including leaving her four school-age boys in the care of others as she pursued a degree in the United States. But now as a grand-mother, as Madam President, Ellen never forgets a birthday and plans her schedule around the high school and college graduations of her many grandchildren, nephews and nieces. Like any mother anywhere around the world, it is the accomplishments of her family of which she is most proud.

I recall the calculations, the decisions, the effort, the brilliance, the flawed ideas, the pleas to friends and supporters, the advocacy in Washington, DC—all the circumstances that ultimately made it possible for her to make history, to become the first elected woman president of an African nation.

I think about her first inauguration, January 26, 2006, when she promised to "make the children smile again," about the race to rebuild the country, its infrastructure, healthcare system, institutions and schools, and about the effort to restore Liberia's economy, settle its debt obligations and to reinstate the country into the community of nations.

I count out the remarkable successes that this post-conflict nation has been able to achieve, but also note the inevitable race against time, a race that very few politicians win, to keep progress going at a greater pace than the heightened expectations of a young and restless population.

The trumpets come to a dramatic halt.

It is time for words. Time to name the deeds that we are here to honor.

Thorbjørn Jagland, the chairman of the Norwegian Nobel Committee, approaches the podium. "All those with empathy for children and women who are ill-treated and killed, all those who believe in a future free from violence and war, will acclaim you today out of respect for the will to act that you represent."

He continues, "You give concrete meaning to the Chinese proverb which says *women hold up half the sky.* That was why, when giving its reasons for this year's award, the Nobel Committee stated that 'We cannot achieve democracy and lasting peace in the world unless women acquire the same opportunities as men to influence developments at all levels of society.' We thank you for the hope you awaken in us all. Luckily women are not only victims. Some take action. Three of them are today receiving the Nobel Peace Prize for 2011."

I am just a spectator but I drink this in like he is talking to me. Then Jagland turns to Liberia and to Ellen.

"Liberia remains one of the poorest countries in the world, and faces huge problems, but much progress has nevertheless been made since Johnson Sirleaf was installed as President in 2006. The civil war is over; democracy is working; there has been considerable economic growth; the very widespread corruption has been somewhat reduced; women's education and participation in social life has been significantly strengthened; the monstrous number of rapes has diminished. Few other persons better satisfy the criteria for receiving the Peace Prize mentioned in Alfred Nobel's will. Congratulations!"

The audience applauds with warmth and heart. After the two other laureates are presented, Ellen is called first among the three to address the world. She wears a rich deep purple African dress with a matching headdress, accompanied by a contrasting crème-colored sash, and her signature pearl jewelry. She looks, as always, regal, confident, proper, and appropriate for a grandmother-president.

I study Ellen's expression and see a great lady preparing to assume a new burden, that of the legacy of the Nobel, one that few in the world are privileged to carry. Moments later, Ellen's words match this sentiment, "History will judge us not by what we say in this moment in time, but by what we do next to lift the lives of our countrymen and women. It will judge us by the legacy we leave behind for generations to come."

Legacy, yes, I think. It is what we leave and how we are remembered that matters. I feel the warmth reclaim my body.

Ellen calls out to her young people, referring especially to those who did not vote for her in her second presidential contest. "We heard the cry of our young population that they are impatient for their lives to improve. They want to make up for the time and opportunities lost during years of conflict and deprivation. They have found their voices, and we have heard them." I sense that Ellen is anxious to return home, to vest her young people in the institutions of democracy she is struggling to build.

Ellen closes her speech with both a plea and an invitation. "I urge my sisters, and my brothers, not to be afraid. Be not afraid to denounce injustice, though you may be outnumbered. Be not afraid to seek peace, even if your voice may be small. Be not afraid to demand peace." There is a poignant silence. I look over at the King of Norway, his tie so perfectly knotted. This is really happening. She continues, "If I might thus speak to girls and women everywhere, I would issue them this simple invitation: My sisters, my daughters, my friends, find your voices."

She has named it — what we all must do, what I too have learned to do over two decades navigating the often treacherous politics from Washington to Monrovia and back.

As I watch Ellen take her bows at the Nobel podium, I look around in disbelief. Who could have imagined back in 1996 that Liberia, a country thought to be irreparably broken, would emerge as a model for post-conflict transformation? But sometimes good does triumph over evil. And yes, the rewards of battling injustice far outweigh the paltry riches of self-interest. Ellen now stands in front of the world as a new model of success for generations of African girls and women. My hands grip the sides of the printed program. I turn my head and meet Jennie's eyes. They are filled with tears. Ellen has given me something worth fighting for, and I returned the deed. I look up and imagine my grandmother's soul looking down from the eaves of this holy town hall.

"Find your voices," I repeat, as Ellen takes her seat.

Letter to Riva following mission to Somalia.

ONE

HE'S OUR BAD GUY

Mogadishu, Somalia
July, 1989

It is the middle of the night, July 27, 1989, and I am aboard an ancient Kenya Airways 707 that was retired long ago from the US fleet. Its stained fuselage riddled with rust spots around the nose and cargo area give away its age and condition. We are flying from Nairobi, Kenya, to Mogadishu, Somalia, and I am feeling decidedly queasy. My complexion matches the faded green hue of the plane seats. As if this ancient aircraft were not enough to worry about, I am traveling to Mogadishu to meet with a murderous dictator. His name is Siad Barre, but he goes by the nickname of "Mighty Mouth."

Human rights organizations, not to mention our own US State Department, have documented a long list of barbaric acts carried out by Barre. An Africa Watch Committee report noted that Somalis under Barre's rule suffered "summary killings, arbitrary arrest, detention in squalid conditions, torture, rape, crippling constraints on freedom of movement and expression and a pattern of psychological intimidation." Barre recently commanded his ruthless cadre of Red Berets—the widely feared *Duub Cas*—to unleash a campaign of terror against rival clans in Northwest Somali Land. Reports are that they bayoneted to death one thousand civilians, the majority of them women and children.

I am going to meet Mighty Mouth in person. Voluntarily.

At this point in my life and career, I am a strategist and international field operative for BMS&K—Black, Manafort, Stone & Kelly—Washington, D.C.'s very first bipartisan lobbying firm. According to a *Newsweek* cover story that year, "BMS&K is the hottest shop in town."

The firm is unique to Washington. It is part politics, part public policy, part commerce, a curious mix of self-interest, selflessness and opportunism that could exist only in our nation's capital. BMS&K gets paid to change policy and alter opinions. Tasks can be something as narrow as a modification of the tax code or as all-encompassing as building strategic alliances against America's enemies, real or perceived.

BMS&K deals in big-ticket items. Following two terms of President Ronald Reagan, we are in an era of proxy wars and freedom fighters, and the world can see the first signs of the impending collapse of the Soviet Union. Foreign governments and political parties are willing to pay us a lot of money to ensure that they are properly allied with the United States. It is a time in global politics when good and evil are easily discerned, as simple as black and white. At least it seems that way to the Reaganites and their successors in the administration of President George H.W. Bush.

◆

After more than 24 hours of travel from Washington, DC, via London and Nairobi with my colleague and friend John Donaldson, we are approaching Mogadishu as dawn breaks. John is of medium height and round build, with curly brown hair and oval glasses, making him a dead ringer for the cartoon character Mr. Magoo. John shares my passion for making a positive difference in the world and possesses a self-effacing charm and wit that make my association with him very enjoyable. He is my best friend in the firm.

We are both bleary-eyed from the long and bumpy ride on this decomposing airliner. We can thank our boss, Paul John Manafort, for our exhaustion. He informed us on Monday that we were going to Africa— and that we were leaving in three days. Paul broke the news to us in his spacious corner office located in historic Old Town Alexandria. The office features a balcony overlooking the Potomac River. Staring at us from the office walls was a bevy of past presidents, US senators, congressmen and other power notables.

"I've heard from El Assir in Paris," Paul told us, referring to his shady Middle Eastern intermediary. "He says the Somali government is prepared to sign a contract."

"To do what?" I asked, mindful of Barre's reputation.

"The usual," Manafort replied. "We'll have a contract ready in an hour."

"But we don't have any visas," John pointed out. "Will there be a facilitator?"

"El Assir will take care of all that," Manafort assured us.

If we were skeptical, we had good reason. The mysterious Abdul Rahman el-Assir would later be accused by French investigators of being one of two middlemen seeking to sell French submarines to Pakistan and then funneling the proceeds to the campaign of French presidential hopeful Édouard Balladur.

Over six feet tall with large brown eyes, a stocky build and dark Italian features, Manafort isn't good looking, precisely, but he does have a commanding presence that compels you to notice him when he walks into a room. He is one of those rare individuals who can cut through the noise, unerringly get to the heart of a problem and hit on a solution. Manafort would later be hired by billionaire Donald Trump to advise him on his 2016 presidential campaign. Inside the firm, we joke that working at BMS&K is like playing one big game of *Stratego*: building armies and scheming to take over the world. That is exactly what it feels like working with Manafort. In fact, at times, that is exactly what is going on.

No doubt John and I were thinking the same thing: better get the malaria pills, make an emergency appointment at Traveler's Medical Service to update our shots, and pray that El Assir comes through. Assuming we get the contract, our job will be to do some emergency revamping of Barre's international image and persuade him to halt his human rights abuses or risk losing US support and ultimately his job, not to say his life, if he doesn't clean up his act. It is not exactly a message that is guaranteed to meet with smiles and handshakes.

Somalia is a desperately poor country situated at the Horn of Africa, across the Red Sea from Yemen. It is one of five countries in Africa colonized by the Italians beginning in the 19th century, and its political and economic development since independence has been a dismal failure. Poverty and corruption are institutionalized. The country played flip-flop between Soviet and US interests during the Cold War, and neither superpower had the slightest idea what to do with the place. But that didn't stop them from trying.

The Soviet Union once tried to spur economic development by building a fish cannery on Somalia's beautiful Indian Ocean coastline. But in a classic example of Soviet mismanagement, the fish guts and refuse dumped back into the once-pristine local waters created a lethal feeding ground for sharks. Somali children would routinely get attacked as they played in the waist-deep surf.

Yet Somalia matters to the US government, and therefore Barre matters, too. Somalia hosts a strategic US naval facility at the mouth of the Red Sea. The neighboring country of Ethiopia is aligned with the Soviets. All over the region, the US and the Soviet Union are engaged in a political turf war. This is why Washington is propping up Barre and providing him with hundreds of millions of dollars in aid—most of it spent on weapons. He relies on US aid to support his war with the Soviet-backed Ethiopian insurgents.

It did not seem like a promising strategy to march into the dictator's office and point out to him and his staff that he has a public relations problem. Mighty Mouth had other priorities.

"Are we sure we want *this* guy as a client?" I asked Manafort, in a garish display of naiveté.

Manafort sounded agitated, as if I had asked the right question at the wrong time. "We all know Barre is a bad guy, Riva. We just have to make sure he's *our* bad guy. Have a great trip."

◆

John drums his fingers on the tray table as he reviews our file on Somalia. "This is a classic Manafort move," he says. "The bigger the problem, the bigger the fee."

I glance over at the contract that Manafort prepared. "Two hundred and fifty thousand dollars up front?"

"That's just a quarter of the charge," John explains.

Sighing, I shake my head and repeat Manafort's words to us: "He's *our* bad guy.'"

"That's our boss," John snickers.

Arrogant, narcissistic, egotistical, brilliant—all of that I can handle in Paul. It is Paul's mercenary attitude that puts us at odds.

It's one thing if you're pitching competing brands of toothpaste to the American consumer; it's another if your clients are players in a global struggle against communism and the consequences of their actions— and yours—can impact thousands of lives. I have to believe in what I'm doing, and I have to believe it's something for the good. That's ingrained in my psyche.

It is also what Manafort predicts will be my downfall in this business.

John continues, "If we can reach the US ambassador at the embassy, we're good. We need to have him sign off on us helping Barre—without causing any conflict with US national security interests. Then we'll meet with Barre and his prime minister. Get the contract signed. Have them wire the money."

We look at each other.

"Two meetings. Two days," I say. "Doesn't sound like Mission Impossible."

Oh, little did we know.

John closes the file, reclines his seat, and slips off his glasses. He'll be out in seconds. It's a gift, his ability to fall asleep quickly, anywhere. Alone now with my thoughts, I have two choices: stare out the window at the rusted wing and pray it doesn't fall off, or review significant life choices to determine how the hell I got to where I am right now, beginning my shaky descent into Mogadishu.

◆

My childhood in Westport, Connecticut, was a long, slow slide from storybook to nightmare. It began with a four-story white colonial house, assorted pets, vacations in Cape Cod, sleepover camp in Maine, a live-in maid. It ended with me as a transient, always dreading the end of the month when the stipend for alimony and child support would run out, leaving no food in the fridge and the telephone bill unpaid. My parents divorced when I was thirteen. My mom's bipolar disease consumed her and defined my existence until college.

From the day of the divorce until the late August morning in 1979 when I left for college, I never brought any of my friends home. If I had, they might have witnessed—as our neighbors did—my mother's manic fits. Tossing all of my clothes into the front yard, for example, or attempting to have me arrested for some imagined crime her faulty brain chemistry convinced her I had committed. The day I was pulled out of my American History class by two uniformed police officers in the middle of my final exam on the Civil War haunted me for years.

How did I, a teenage girl with a bipolar mother and a distant father, cope? I pretended I was just like everyone else. I would show up every morning at Staples High School with my game face on. I became a varsity cheerleader. I obsessed about grades. I went out for the school musicals, school government, the yearbook—anything that kept me in school until dark. I also had a plan: seek early admission to any college that would give me a scholarship.

Mom's illness was a terrible burden for all of us, but my dad had his own issues. A child of the great depression, he seemed to live in wait of impending financial ruin. After the bitter, two-year breakup, he became obsessed with keeping score. He was left with a legal financial obligation to my mother and to us kids. If something wasn't expressly written into the 42-page agreement, he wouldn't pay for it—not school supplies, not sports equipment, not a prom dress, not even my appendectomy—nothing. The divorce papers also said that he didn't have to assume any financial responsibilities after we children turned 18. My dad took that literally, too—no college tuition, not even a weekly food stipend.

It would take me a long time to forgive my dad for what felt like abandonment. But I did, eventually. He wanted some happiness in his life, and he took the escape clause. I understand that now. My dad's scorekeeping was his own coping mechanism. He didn't love me any less; it was a survival skill.

Forgiving my mother would be a more complex task. It would take time, space—and Oma.

Without Oma, I don't know if any of us would have made it—my twin, Kenny, my sister, Kim, or my youngest brother, Kevan. Oma—her full name was Manja Pakter Kroner—was my mother's mother. Born on October 30, 1900, she beat all the odds. Despite being a woman and a Jew, Oma became a physician in Germany at the height of anti-Semitism. She was fortunate enough to study for a time under Albert Einstein, one of the many intellectuals who warned her to leave Germany while she still could.

Oma was barely five feet when held straight by the brace that protected her spine from degenerating osteoporosis. She had the deepest-set, brown-black eyes that always seemed to be wide open, even when she smiled. While age had taken its toll on her small sturdy body, it seemed to have no effect on her memory and the clarity of her thinking. She also retained the most beautiful youthful skin.

Oma fled to America on July 4, 1936, aboard the USS *Manhattan*, along with her husband, Jacques, also a doctor, my mother Edith and my mother's sister, Eleanor. My grandmother left behind her parents and eight siblings. She tried to convince them to flee with her, but they were adamant: "This is our home." All perished in the Holocaust.

My grandmother lived to the age of 87. Oma was in the care of a nursing home in the Bronx when she slipped on the wet bathroom floor and broke her leg. She had gone blind from glaucoma and was forced to vacate her Manhattan apartment of 50 years on 35 West 92nd Street, one block from Central Park. It depressed her not to be able to read, so she passed the time with her tape recorder and books on cassettes.

My grandmother never quite accepted television as a means to be entertained and educated. Truth is, she never quite accepted the new world, as she called it. She was a conflicted woman. She pined for a return to the history, culture and art of Europe. But at the same time, she refused to speak the German language after the day she learned of her family's fate, even though Germany had once been her home too.

I visited my grandmother for the last time on a gray, wet, foggy January afternoon a few weeks before she died. Her leg was in traction, raised 45 degrees from her shrunken body. She was in great pain and held in her left hand a crumpled piece of tissue between her ring and pinky fingers to wipe her tears. She always held a tissue in her left hand, between her fourth and pinky finger, tears or not. It has become my habit now.

She shared a small hospital room with another elderly woman. They were separated by a yellow curtain with turquoise flowers. Every time my grandmother would moan in pain, the other lady would tell her to shut up. I had talked to the management about moving my grandmother, but they told me that there were no other rooms.

"Oma, it's Riva." I bent over my grandmother and kissed her forehead, cold and damp with perspiration. I held onto the hand with the tissue.

To my grandmother, I had been Riva since the day I was born. She was dead set against the American names my mother chose to give her grandchildren—Kim, Kenneth, Kevan, all Ks, including mine, Karen. Oma insisted that all of us have middle names tied to her family in Europe. Riva was the name of her eldest sister. "Riva, darling, thank you for coming," my grandmother said in her beautiful accent, a mixture of Polish, Russian, and German.

She then let out a moan of agony, which was followed by a "Shut up!" from the other side of the yellow curtain. I never opened the curtain. I did not want to see that woman's face.

"I have something to ask of you, Riva," Oma said.

"Anything," I replied.

"Your life has not been easy with your mother's illness. And I know how much pain she has caused you with her behavior. But I ask you to remember, please, that she cannot help herself. Know that if she could have been the perfect mother, she would have been."

"She is so hard on me. Sometimes I get so angry," I replied, recalling the night before when my mother had telephoned me collect 13 times until I finally had to take the phone off the hook.

"Promise me that no matter what happens, you will always take care of your mother. Please don't let your anger smother the love I know you have in your heart," pleaded my grandmother.

She let out another moan, which was followed by another "Shut up!"

"I promise you," I said, tears streaming down my face.

Those were the final words my grandmother and I exchanged. Gangrene later set in from her prolonged sedentary state. She died soon thereafter.

During my intermittent moments of certainty, when I am not second-guessing my major life decisions, I find peace by thinking of myself first and foremost as my grandmother's granddaughter. I am determined to honor her memory, always.

Back in the summer of 1985, after graduating from college and working for two years at a nonprofit organization, waiting on tables at night, and teaching aerobics during my lunch hours, I still did not have enough money to get by. Oma was concerned about me. She urged me to leave D.C. and come live with her in New York City. Certainly it would be easier to find a job in Manhattan, she would say on our weekly calls, and I would not need to worry about rent or transportation. It was a tempting offer. I was on the verge of accepting.

But then I got my big break: I landed a job with Paul Manafort.

◆

It was 95 degrees on the afternoon of July 19, 1985, when I arrived for my job interview, sweat-soaked from the ride in my un-air-conditioned 1975 Oldsmobile Omega. The driver's-side door was broken so I had to squeeze out the passenger side. I parked far enough away so that no one of importance would witness this embarrassing maneuver.

Lobbying firms are notorious for only hiring from within—either offspring of high-placed government insiders or successful campaign strategists. None of that was on my resume. I had graduated *magna cum laude* from Tufts University, worked for two years at the Caribbean Council, and had the character-building experience, as I called it, of waiting tables and teaching aerobics.

"Why do you want to work at BMS&K?" Manafort asked.

"Because I've done my research," I answered. "Your company is poised to take off in the international arena and I want to be there. You have projects in Latin America. I speak Spanish. You need someone who has communications skills. I'm a strong writer and a quick study."

Then I uttered those fateful words. "And there's no place I won't go!"

He just stared at me, bemused.

Manafort hired me the next week. Oma was disappointed not to have my company in New York, but thrilled that I finally got a break. I became Manafort's Third World traveler of choice. As I promised in the job interview, there was no place I wouldn't go. And there was no place Manafort wouldn't send me.

◆

The plane lurches as we begin our descent and John's eyelids pop open. He puts his hand protectively on my arm, sensing my distress. It's not so much about this mission or being a passenger on this rickety plane, but thoughts of my disintegrating personal life back home. A relationship, a serious one—or so I hoped. But now I am not so sure. I am filled with doubt about my future and the man I thought I would spend it with. I am happy to get out of DC for a while, even relieved to get some distance. But maybe not *this* kind of distance. I am about to land in Somalia where now, as the collision between clans intensifies, chaos and rampant violence are consuming the nation. In fact, a loosely aligned group of rebels is rumored to be nearing Mogadishu this very day.

John reaches into his bag and pulls out a well-worn book on Somalia. As is his habit before arriving at any destination, John briefs me on the history of the country, the culture and the obscure facts that delight him no end.

"The hatred between the clans in Somalia is ironic," he says, "because they believe they're all descended from one man, their mythical founder, Samaale."

I nod politely. I can't muster up my usual enthusiasm for John's encyclopedic mind. Not only am I nauseated from this flight, I'm focused on my boyfriend Eddy's last words before I left for Africa: "You're 90 percent what I want, but there's still ten percent that weighs on me."

My mind has been racing wildly with scrambled thoughts attempting to figure out what the missing ten percent is. *Do I need to gain, or lose, ten pounds? Up my IQ by ten points?* This is ridiculous thinking, I know. I'm in love with Eddy. I'm 28. We've been together for six years. Naturally, I've envisioned our wedding and our kids. A legislative assistant for a highly regarded Republican Congressman, Eddy is handsome in the John Kennedy, Jr. mold. He shares my love of sports, laughs at my stupid jokes. Even more, his family has become my own, offering me a kind of support and love that my own family never could. Maybe if I could splice off ten percent of my genes and clean up the pool of instability that resides in my family's muddled history…

To hell with Eddy. I'm not an equation.

As we land in Mogadishu, the rattling noise of the 707's engines seems to echo the confusion in my brain. With a sinking feeling, I look out the window and see nothing but mud and clouds of dust. We taxi along the runway and the terminal, a squat, one-story, filthy white cinderblock building, comes into view. John and I peer out the window and get a first glimpse of the city's unique brand of pandemonium. Local men and boys swarm the airport. The government security forces, dressed in dirty khaki fatigues, stand by, heavily armed. As for tourists, there appear to be only two. The rest of the travelers are merchants moving goods between Kenya and Somalia. Here in the wartime economy, the mark-up for everything from candy bars to weapons will be huge.

I turn to John and ask, "John, honestly, do you think this is a good idea?"

"Probably not," he answers.

As we walk down the metal steps to the tarmac, my eyes scan the jostling crowd for someone holding a handwritten sign with our names, or BMS&K, scrawled on it. When it works, here's the drill: a facilitator—possibly armed—is supposed to meet us at the gate. He'll help get our money exchanged, protect us from marauding opportunists, pay off whatever airport officials need to be bribed in order to get our luggage, escort us to a waiting car, and safely deposit us at the hotel. This is pretty routine procedure in most of the African countries we travel to, and we hope that it is going to happen without a hitch.

The September heat and the equatorial humidity hit us like a punch to my already nauseated gut. There is no sign, and there is no facilitator. El Assir's absence adds to the punch and the sweat already seeping through my clothes. We move inside the receiving building where the heat is stifling and the air is teeming with malaria-infested mosquitoes. We walk down a narrow hallway past soldier after soldier, their AK-47s dangling as lazily as their cigarettes. The locals, mostly men, size us up with calculating, unfriendly eyes. They speak rapid, hushed Italian—still the predominant language of Somalia—scheming, to my mind, an easy ambush of two displaced and seemingly helpless white people.

Please be here. Please be here. This is my prayer as I try desperately to conjure the physical manifestation of El Assir, our invisible facilitator. I direct my plea to any god who happens to be listening, even Samaale, the founding father of this forsaken, dysfunctional land.

On the way to baggage claim, we stop to exchange dollars for Somali shillings. One hundred US dollars equals more than 200,000 shillings. Luckily, we've anticipated needing to haul lots of money around, so we've both brought empty satchels for the purpose. Hauling those bags now fat with hundreds of thousands of shillings, I feel we are truly one giant invitation to assault and robbery. Or worse.

We are stopped by an old man in a yellow-stained lab coat. He demands to see our inoculation cards. Hardly glancing at them, he pulls dirty, rusted needles from his medicine bag and tells us we have to have more shots.

This is not going to happen. For 40,000 shillings, he goes away.

We approach the baggage counter where our luggage is in plain sight. Of course, it has been opened. Pieces of clothing are now trapped in the zippers. Anything considered valuable is undoubtedly no longer there. This is but another "routine procedure." As a rule, we never check bags for this very reason, but the Kenyan Airways authorities gave us no choice.

John takes the lead and hands our claim tickets to a surly male attendant. Behind him, other attendants smoke and exchange private jokes in Italian. We are told that we have to pay a "processing fee."

John dips into his parcel of shillings and pays the man, who turns to his colleagues and ignores us. John reaches for more shillings and deposits them on the counter. Now it seems that John and I are the invisible ones, and not just our facilitator.

"Possiamo avere nostro bagaglio, prego?" I ask.

May we have our luggage, please?

John looks at me as if I've just sprouted antlers.

"You speak Italian?"

"Spanish," I say, "but I dated an Italian once."

There's no other way to explain how the language flew out of my mouth, as if I were channeling Emilio, my European fling from a few years ago.

But we're still getting no reaction. *"Abbastranza soldi. I nostri sacchetti, per favore,"* I say firmly.

Enough money. Luggage, please.

The attendant looks at us with a surprised smile.

"Over here," he says, pointing to our suitcases. He directs John to step inside the secured, cordoned-off area. As John grabs our bags, the attendant, indicating me, says to his buddies, *"Moglie esigente. Povero uomo."*

Demanding wife. Poor man.

Hastily making our way toward the exit, I turn to John and ask, "Am I too demanding?"

"Strong-willed," he answers with a smile. "Not demanding."

I scope out the situation as John puts our bags into the trunk of a waiting yellow taxi that is missing the passenger side door and all the windows except for the windshield. I catch the driver signaling to two men who linger at the airport exit. In a split-second, I can see it: They'll take us to Lido Beach and shoot us, which is, in this moment, what I would like to do to Manafort.

Paying attention to nuanced signals is my specialty, and I can thank my mom for this. She could turn on a dime, flip from happy to savage in an instant. Early on I learned to watch for the tiniest clue that could ignite her—an angry look from a neighbor, a dog barking incessantly, a news broadcast that she disagreed with. When danger was coming I knew it intuitively, and I would seek refuge at a friend's house.

John starts to climb into the backseat.

"Get out, John! Not this car!" I look squarely into the face of the driver, who avoids my gaze. "Open the trunk, we need our bags," I order him. To John I whisper, "It's a set-up." I nod toward the two men waiting at the exit.

"Good catch, Riva," John says, wide-eyed.

Like vultures, other drivers descend on our bags. Using my newly reborn Italian, I finally settle on a driver who, I'm 50 percent convinced, won't put a gun to our heads. Before leaving Nairobi, I studied a map of Mogadishu, paying special attention to the easiest, safest route from the airport to the city. The only paved road in all of Mogadishu is the airport runway. Instructing our driver to follow my directions, I notice he becomes increasingly agitated. When I ask a question, he turns slightly and directs his answer to John, not me. Finally, at an intersection where we are stopped, he turns fully to John and says, "Please tell lady not to address me, it's embarrass."

Keeping my mouth shut, I pass my map to John. The driver is Muslim and not accustomed to a woman telling him what to do. He is right to communicate his distress. These are his beliefs, and I am in his country.

As we enter the city, the *cariishes*—structures that most Somalis call home—are striking. These rectangular houses built from mud, sometimes mixed with cow dung, typically have just three rooms in which more than a dozen people often live together in squalor. Mothers and fathers struggle to provide even a single meal a day for their families. But even so, we see young children, barefoot and unwashed, with protruding bellies, laughing and playing in the streets, oblivious to their plight. Oxen lumber down the road and chickens crisscross in front of our moving vehicle. John says the animals' owners track their every movement. I can't see how that is possible. We pass crowded outdoor markets selling cassava, assorted vegetables, game and fish, lots of cigarettes, and—for those who can afford them—peanuts and honey-encrusted sweets.

"Ah, a *xabadsooda* store," John remarks gleefully as we pass a weary, sagging structure. "Traditional medicines for all sicknesses except death," he explains. "They even have cures for *mingis*," he says. "Spirit possession."

"Good to know," I reply. "I left my possession medicine at home."

At last we arrive at our destination: the Hotel Guled, soon to become infamous as the structure marking the "Guled Line" in the impending civil war. There is no star rating that applies to a hotel such as this, in a city such as this. If there were, maybe minus four. Even minus five.

All around Mogadishu there is a disturbing, unsettled feeling, as if the whole city is somehow off-kilter—perhaps possessed is the right word. You get the sense that the whole place might detonate at any moment. I feel it in the streets, I can see it in the eyes of the men, young and old. Suspicion, fear and a simmering anger, as tangible as the soot and the rancid stench in the air.

I settle into my hotel room and eye the thick, frayed electrical power cords snaking in through an open window. My guess is that the hotel is siphoning power from some other source. There's no showerhead in my bathroom, but at least I have a bathroom. The bed creaks, but at least it's a bed. I am quickly learning the art of the "glass half full" outlook, a useful tool in Somalia. The walls are a canvas of sprawling, splotchy stains. I am reminded of being a child, staring at clouds and seeing fantastic things, like elephants, angels, ice-cream cones. One wall-stain bears an unsettling resemblance to Richard Nixon, in profile.

Later at a thatched-roof café nearby, we hungrily anticipate our first meal in 36 hours. The waiter appears with a steaming loaf of bread—one of my passions. When I split a piece open, I discover dozens of dead brown bugs embedded in the bread.

"Waiter," I say sweetly, "there's a bug in my bread." It sounds like the straight-guy line in a bad joke.

The waiter is tall and too thin, with skin so dark it is difficult to make out his features. He wears a white jacket buttoned to his neck. He expresses extreme regret and spirits the bread away to the kitchen. We soon hear peals of laughter. He returns with another loaf. Not so eager this time, I tear off a tiny piece and a bread bug stares back at me.

Now John begins to laugh.

"Riva," he says, "all the wheat in Somalia is infested with bugs. They're added protein."

Perhaps Mr. Magoo could have shared this cultural gem with me earlier.

Back in my hotel room, I gaze out the only window as a warm, gentle rain begins to fall. Within minutes, it becomes a steamy deluge. Rivulets of water trickle down the wall, right over Richard Nixon's brow. All at once, the deluge increases and slanting streaks of rain blast the ground like gunfire. Instantly, a river of water has obliterated the road. My wall is now a waterfall and the electrical cords drip like wet, menacing snakes.

I wonder if I will be electrocuted. Perhaps the rapidly rising river below my window will flood the hotel, sweeping John and me away. Or maybe the rebel forces steadily marching toward Mogadishu will arrive and just kill us for the crime of being foreigners in this very wrong place at this very wrong time. My outlook has flipped to "glass half empty."

Our phone calls to Barre and his associates have yet to be returned. We have no meeting scheduled. Reports claim that rebel forces continue to advance and an outbreak of violence is imminent. On the level of basic human needs, I am so hungry, I'd eat a bread bug right now. Sleep isn't likely to come, thanks to the deafening sound of the monsoon. Eddy springs to mind again. I picture him all cozy in our bed back in the apartment in Georgetown, mulling over the missing ten percent of me that weighs on him.

I may never forgive Manafort for this.

At dawn, the dark clouds disperse, disappearing like a bad dream, yet giving way to what will soon become a living nightmare.

John arrives at my door looking as wrecked as I do. He hands me a cup of thick Somali coffee and tells me that President Barre is unavailable, but we have secured a meeting with the prime minister for tomorrow, the day we're scheduled to leave. Meanwhile, we are due at the US embassy in an hour. No guarantee we can see the ambassador, but someone will receive us.

As we review our game plan, I begin to hear a faint buzzing sound. It seems to be growing louder. What is wrong with my hearing? I rub my ears. Then I notice John rubbing his.

"What is that sound?" I ask, annoyed.

John's eyes widen in horror. He races to the window and quickly tries to close it, but the power cords keep it from shutting completely. He grabs a pillow and frantically stuffs it into the window opening. That's when I see them—twisting tornadoes of black bugs the size of golf balls swarm through the air, blotting out the sun. They splat and crack against the window, millions upon millions of them spreading across the sky, as if they were sent by some vengeful god to demolish the city and drive out its inhabitants. The buzzing has grown into a high-pitched roar. I feel as if I've been thrust into a B horror movie.

"Holy shit!" John cries out, backing away from the window.

"What is this, a plague?" I ask. "The monsoon. Now locusts? This is biblical!"

"They're mayflies," he says. "*Ephemeroptera.* They come out of their cocoons for one day. That's their life-span—twenty-four hours."

No, no, I think. A mayfly is a tiny bug, the kind of insect that fly fisherman tie onto their hooks. These creatures are monsters, prehistoric ancestors of nothing that could reasonably be called a mayfly.

"You'll only see this once in your life," John proclaims with authority.

"Promise?" I say, shaken at the prospect of walking outside into this insect apocalypse. For a moment, we stand silent and helpless, surrounded by the awful sound of brief existence, and worry about our own.

Draped in bed sheets and wielding wooden coat hangers from our hotel closet, John and I plunge outside and battle our way through the swarming mass. No mayfly invasion—even giant Somali mayflies—is going to keep us from our lunch meeting with the US ambassador. For the moment, the locals seem relieved to have a diversion from the trial of their everyday lives. "They'll eat them," John shouts as we make a dash for our ride. "They're considered a delicacy!"

The embassy has mercifully sent a car for us. By the time we arrive for our meeting, the insect hordes have thinned from unbearable to merely deeply disturbing. The US Embassy is situated in the heart of downtown Mogadishu on a narrow, mud-baked street that clouds with dust every time a car passes by. A block away is the building that houses the United States Information Agency (USIA). These are the two sturdiest buildings in the city, by far, and the only ones with visible air-conditioning units and uniformed security.

Once through the security checkpoint, we take seats in a small waiting area. We are deeply grateful for the cool air free of monster mayflies. We engage in conversation a local Embassy employee, a tall, stately woman named Ashra. She has the mix of Arabic and African lineage that characterizes many Somalis, who are known for their elongated bodies, narrow faces and long, elegant features. Her head is covered with a purple *hijab*, which complements her colorful floor-length dress. She has a pleasant demeanor, deep-set black eyes and a welcoming smile.

"The embassy and the USIA building will be closed within six months," she informs us. "All US personnel will be moved to the new embassy building, near Lido Beach. No more living and working among the local population for the Americans," she continues. "They believe it has become too dangerous. I don't know if I will keep my position. The new embassay is far from the city and I do not have access to transport."

John and I are moved by her plight, but we have nothing to offer, not even reassurances. Mohammed, the Somali driver who brought us here, was also very upset by the decision. "This is the only place where we can mingle with US and other international citizens, where we can freely exchange ideas, discuss and debate." "When it is closed, we will be even more isolated."

Twenty minutes later, we are ushered in to meet a political officer named Mike Newman. He is dressed in a short-sleeved shirt with his tie loosened. Even with the air-conditioning, he's sweating from the scorching heat. "Unfortunately, the ambassador cannot meet with you today," he states flatly.

"We understand," I say, hoping I am successful in hiding the annoyance I feel. We are 0 for 2 so far, and batting zero.

"We're here in Mogadishu to sign a contract with President Barre," John explains. "Our firm plans to lobby for the Somali government in Washington."

"We're well aware of the human rights violations by this government," I add quickly. "If we get the contract, we'll tell President Barre that he's got to change these practices in order to keep his American support."

"I see," Newman replies. He looks unimpressed by our announcement and skeptical of our chances. "It's really your company's choice whether you lobby for this government or not," he continues. "My only advice to you is: get paid in advance."

"What do you mean by that?" I ask, my voice rising. John and I are a bit stunned by his comment, but we do our best to hide it.

"This government is losing its grip on the country. It controls Mogadishu, but beyond the capital, rebel soldiers are beating the government forces and grabbing more territory every day. Officially, we support the Barre government—that is, as long as the Barre government still exists."

Back at the hotel, it is dusk now. The mayflies, mercifully less in number, continue their writhing dance. In the fading light, they look like large, undulating shadows. I've grown almost used to their noise. As I drift off to sleep, I find that it helps to quiet the swarm of worried thoughts in my brain.

The next morning, John and I approach the hotel clerk to settle our bill—in cash, of course.

"It's a good thing you're leaving today," says Mustafa, the soft-spoken 16-year-old Egyptian clerk whose father owns the hotel. "The rebels are only 60 kilometers from the center of town."

"What will you do if they come?" I ask.

"What we've done before. Try to be a safe haven for foreigners and a neutral zone for the opposing sides." Mustafa hands me a chocolate bar with Arabic lettering and the face of a male lion on its wrapper.

"You look like you could use it," he says. "It is from Egypt."

"Thank you," I say, touched by this small act of generosity amidst the growing uncertainty around us.

"Is there going to be an evacuation?" John interjects. "When should we get to the airport?"

"At least four hours early," Mustafa answers. "Bring much currency. If the prime minister's office can send someone with you, you will be more likely to keep your seats on your plane."

Likely to keep our seats? I repeat to myself. We wish Mustafa luck and he wishes us the same. Leaving the hotel, we find ourselves walking on a blanket of dead mayflies. Their carcasses are everywhere. It sounds like breaking glass when we step on them. And it feels like an omen.

We decide that I will go to the airport with our luggage while John tries to complete a quick meeting with President Barre's prime minister, maybe even get the contract signed. Otherwise, the trip will turn out to be a total failure. John and I are both pale, even a little green around the edges. But the good news is we're leaving.

At least, that's what we assumed.

The chaos at the airport now looks like a human reenactment of yesterday's mayfly invasion. Swarms of panicked Somalis and other would-be travelers surround anyone who looks like an airport official or even someone with reliable information. The babble of pleas and threats and oaths is deafening. You can taste the fear in the air. For the first time, I admit to myself that I am on the edge of losing it.

I have never been more determined to get on a plane in my life. But then I find out the worst. I wade into a throng of shouting men and women and catch a few phrases from a thin, sweating airport official who looks as if he fears for his life. There is no plane. It does not exist. Or rather, it did exist, but not anymore. The man John and I came here to meet, the man who was supposed to sign our contract and become our client, President Said Barre, has taken our plane. He has commandeered our Somali Air 707 and is on his way to Libya to get more weapons to fight the rebel forces, who are at the city gates.

We are toast.

Racing over to a small, dirty lean-to that advertises private charters, I am greeted by a sign on the door: "Closed." Of course. What did I expect? First, the missing facilitator, El Assir. Then the omen of the mayfly plague. Now the commandeered airplane. I begin to feel weak from hauling our bags around, and sweat coats my body. I drag myself from one airline to the next, pleading, cajoling, demanding a flight out, and each time being turned away.

I decide to leave the mayhem of the airport and head back downtown to try my luck at the office of Somali Air. When I arrive, a stranded journalist from the BBC whispers to me that there just may be a flight to Egypt leaving—and I should get a seat while I still have a chance.

Out of breath, my hair and clothes both matted to my body, I approach a Somali Air attendant. He is over six feet tall, mustached and unsmiling, yet wearing a clean uniform shirt. I am grateful for this sign of order and authority. His eyes hint at kindness.

It's time to pull out the big guns: cold, hard cash and full-on flirtation.

"Siete la mia soltanto speranza," I breathe.

You are my only hope.

I tell him that I must be on a flight today. I place my satchel of money on the counter between us, casually opening it to further entice him.

Craning back my head because he's more than a foot taller, I gaze into his eyes as tears brim in mine. They are real.

"Realmente to bisogno del vostro aiuto," I whisper.

I really need your help.

He finally smiles—a sweet, largely toothless grin that makes me want to weep.

I score two tickets on a Somali Air flight to Cairo, then to Rome, and on to Frankfurt. We'll figure out a flight to Washington later. I shove all my cash at him and pull out my corporate credit card to pay the difference. I tell him to charge whatever it costs—I don't give a shit. Just get me out of Somalia.

I haven't had contact with John since early this morning, so possessed have I been with getting us a flight out. I forget that John has no idea what's going on, where I am, or that we have a new plan. There are only a dozen working landlines in the country, so telephoning is probably useless. I race back to the hotel, desperate to find him. He's not there. I try to get through to the prime minister's office on the hotel phone, but there's no answer. The clock is ticking. We have to get on that plane.

I rush back to the besieged airport. I pace now in front of the terminal, mobbed by panicked people desperate to escape what will very soon become a battlefield. I am so stressed that I have surely just burned away ten years of my life. What if John doesn't come in time? What if something has happened to him, a rebel attack or a kidnapping or a car accident or... I deliberately avoid looking at my watch. I don't want to know how much time we have. Could I get on that plane without him? Could I bear to stand in this hellish airport and watch our plane take off without me? What would John do in my place? I know what he would do. He would wait for me. Or grab a taxi and go find me, somehow. But he would never leave me in Mogadishu, Somalia.

I look across the sea of people, praying that John's smiling face will appear any second now. He'll be waving a signed contract in his hand. Our Somali nightmare will have a happy ending. Mission successful.

At last, John appears. I shout and wave, jumping up and down like a child. He struggles to make his way through the mob. He can barely walk.

"Oh, God, I thought you'd left," he gasps, and sinks to the ground. "I'm awfully sick."

"I would never leave you here," I reassure him. "Remember our rule—what happens to you happens to me. We're in this together. "

John doesn't smile. He is ghostly white and shivering.

I make him drink some water. I douse a tissue and wipe his brow. He's burning up. Is it food poisoning? Not that I really care right now, but I ask anyway, "Did the prime minister sign our contract?"

John sighs and hangs his head. "He said he would do it tomorrow. We know what tomorrow means here."

Mission failed. Now we would have to try again. Another trip, another time. I would sooner eat a plate full of mayflies than come back here.

Suddenly, a white airliner with the navy blue Somali Air logo taxis into view. It is a beautiful, shimmering jewel. I think, Where in the world did they steal this airplane? And then I think, Who the hell cares?

We clutch our boarding passes as if our survival depends upon it—which it does. We look at all of those people standing in the ticket line, the ones who failed to secure a seat. The distress in that the terminal is more suffocating than the heat.

I help John to his feet and we make it up the steps slowly. Inside the plane everything is clean and shiny. Settled in our seats, I get extra blankets and pillows from the sharply dressed flight attendants and try to make John comfortable, although it is clear that he is in agony.

Finally, I feel the lift. "Wheels up!" I announce to John. We're going home. John gives me weak smile and passes out.

Not me, not a chance. My adrenaline is pumping so strong, I may never sleep again, and I am starving. The flight attendant, dressed in a clean and pressed uniform, a beautiful, reassuring sign, hands me a plastic tray. Next to grilled chicken slathered in some unidentifiable sauce is a roll. Bread. Manna from heaven. Shrink-wrapped in plastic, airtight, pure. There's butter, too. I tear the wrapper off and cut the bread in half and see bugs. Dead. Brown. Bugs.

I look down at John in his feverish slumber. I realize now that to men like Manafort, the world really is one huge game of *Stratego*, and they play to win. The consequences are secondary. Manafort sent John and me on this wild goose chase, this utterly pointless mission, one that could have killed us both, simply because he *could*.

I will have to figure things out. When I get back to Virginia, I will march into Paul's office and insist that I never again be sent on any pointless missions. I will tell him that from now on, I will have a say in what I do and where I travel and what country and leader I chose to support! My choices, my actions will have a positive effect on peoples' lives! I will be the woman that Oma always believed I could be!

I will then hope that he doesn't fire me on the spot.

Our Somalia trip has been a disaster. I see that now, as the large, safe airliner climbs to cruising altitude and heads for Cairo. But from the glass-half-full point of view, this trip was also a huge wake-up call for me. And now that I am fully awake, I am determined to make some changes in my life and work. Big changes, momentous changes.

It's just that I have no idea yet what they will be.

◆

Postscript: Siad Barre was forced into exile in 1991. In 1992, US Marines landed in Mogadishu ahead of a UN Peacekeeping Force to restore order and safeguard relief efforts. Their mission to feed the hungry turned tragic when rival clans, infiltrated by Al Qaeda elements, killed 23 US Marines and dragged their mutilated bodies through the streets of Mogadishu. Viewers from around the world witnessed the massacre live on CNN. The incident became known around the world as "Black Hawk Down."

After the Americans eventually withdrew, 550,000 Somalis—six percent of the population—died of starvation, and 400,000 were displaced during the 16 years of civil war that followed Barre's ouster.

The US military did not return to Africa for another decade. This time the country was Liberia. The year was 2003. US Marines helped force into exile another murderous warlord, this one named Charles Taylor, and paved the way for democratic elections.

That event would lead to a defining moment in my life and career.

(top) John Donaldson in middle on mission in Nicaragua, December 1989.
(bottom) Observing South Africa's first All-Race Election, April 27, 1994.

TWO

WHAT AFRICA COULD BE

New York City
July, 1996

Behind the oversized glasses, his eyes give no hint of warmth or engagement. He seldom smiles, and when he does, it looks strained, like those muscles have not been put to the test in some time. There is a sadness etched in the dark lines of his face, as if he has witnessed great sorrow. It occurs to me that, yes, he has not only witnessed that sorrow, but has caused some of it as well. I address him as Mr. President. He accepts this and all gestures of deference naturally, as if they are his right by birth. His Excellency President Teodoro Obiang Nguema Mbasogo of the Republic of Equatorial Guinea.

Nearly a decade into my career in international public relations, this is not what I had hoped or expected to be doing, acting as personal chaperone for yet another African strongman, hoping to convince the world that democracy has taken root in his tiny, impoverished but recently oil-rich nation. But that is my assignment for BMS&K.

It is Africa after the fall of the Berlin Wall, where the leaders, all men and mostly unelected, recognize that to maintain foreign assistance from the world's Western democracies in this new world order, democratic principles must be introduced into society. However, with no experience in political openness, little political will and weak, failing or non-existent institutions, elections held under pressure deliver exactly what one would expect: a new veneer, with power as entrenched as it was before. So it was for Equatorial Guinea.

After overthrowing his uncle in a bloody coup d'état in 1979, Obiang appeared a more enlightened ruler than his brutal predecessor, and many agreed, including Equatorial Guinea's former colonial power, Spain. There were some notable movements towards democracy, such as a new constitution with provisions for popular elections. But the former was often disregarded and the latter less a democratic process, and more political theater, as in 1989, when Obiang was re-elected overwhelmingly. He was also the only candidate.

Then in 1992, opposition parties were allowed to form, a big step for Equatorial Guinea and Central Africa at the time. Long-awaited multiparty presidential elections were scheduled for February 25, 1996. These elections could have been a turning point for the country, an opening for a president in search of international legitimacy and approval, a sign of hope for an isolated and largely illiterate population of less than one million with a GDP growth soon to explode with the discovery of petroleum off the coast. But they weren't; and it wasn't.

For a brief time I thought I was making good progress. A new beginning was possible, I told myself. The Equatoguinean constitution called for a plurality not a majority of the total votes to win the presidency, and given tribal loyalties, with the president's Fang tribe comprising the largest share of the population, Obiang could legitimately win a free and fair election. It was almost mathematically impossible for him to lose.

In November of 1995, with the February elections looming, I met with the president and his minister for state affairs at the presidential palace on the island capital of Malabo. The palace is designed like the summer residences for the royals in Spain—white stucco walls, orange clay tile roofs, encircled by manicured gardens, the complex just yards off the Atlantic Coast. With the sea breeze wafting through the open windows, the President and his advisor appeared to be listening intently as I made my pitch.

"Mr. President, a viable political opposition is a good thing, for you and for your country. It is a sign of strength, not a sign of weakness. Look at President Clinton in my country. He was just re-elected to the presidency with less than 50 percent of the national vote. America is a stronger country for such a competitive race, especially in the eyes of the international community."

Both men nodded, sagely. I took that as a good sign. Next I petitioned President Obiang to adopt some international best practices of free and fair multiparty elections—specifically, to permit credible international institutions to observe the pre-election environment and the conduct of the election itself. He agreed.

I thought to myself, I have done it! I have helped the President and his minister get past mentality of *winner take all.*

After much back and forth, a team from the Washington, DC-based International Foundation for Elections Systems (IFES) was formed and then credentialed by the government to travel to the country. IFES is the premier non-government institution that provides technical assistance to emergent democracies. Most of its funding comes from the US government, its board members prominent and bi-partisan. IFES's willingness to engage could be seen as a breakthrough.

But while the president and his minister of state agreed on IFES, it appeared that no one else in the government, including the security forces, got the memo. The observer teams were prevented from moving freely, the electoral census was perceived as lacking any credibility, the opposition leaders had limited mobility, and they were given no access to the media. The final straw was that the national electoral commission insisted that there be a public vote—that is, no secret ballot, an essential element in the free expression of the voter's will.

The final IFES report, though offering helpful recommendations going forward, was damning. "The IFES team found that virtually all of the basic elements that guarantee a 'free and fair' election by international standards were in question."

Despite my self-applause for getting IFES into the country, we still ended up with an election result that was disregarded by the international community. Ninety-eight percent of the vote went to the incumbent president, with his party retaining 99 of the 100 seats in parliament. These were not the statistical results I was hoping for. But maybe that had been the plan all along, and I was the one who never got the memo.

So here I am, back in New York, attempting to sell the unsellable. Worse, the supposed buyer is a fearless opposition leader and democratic activist in her own African country of Liberia. I know a few things about

Ellen Johnson Sirleaf, although I have never met her in person. Currently she is the Africa Director for the United Nations Development Program (UNDP), the highest UN post for Africa. Her position is the equivalent of an assistant secretary general, with oversight for the entire development budget for the continent. She is in exile after her fight for human rights and democratic freedom landed her in prison for 18 months and exposed her to years of death threats and harassment. War and unrest have engulfed the country for nearly a decade. It is rumored that Ellen Johnson Sirleaf is intent on returning home to help restore peace.

◆

I know a bit about Liberia from my high school teacher, Mr. Richards. It is "the anomaly of an African nation," Mr. Richards was fond of saying. "The single country on the continent not colonized by Europeans, but by American slaves." I think we were the only American history class at Staples High in Westport, Connecticut that learned about Liberia. Mr. Richards was my favorite high school teacher.

Liberia is located on the western belly of the African continent, with nine of its fifteen counties adjacent to the Atlantic Coast. The country is bordered by Côte d'Ivoire to the southeast, Sierra Leone to the west and Guinea to the north. "It's a tough neighborhood," Mr. Richards would point out, "on an unsettled continent."

The capital of Liberia, Monrovia, was named after then-President James Monroe who supported the American Colonization Society's 1820 plan to resettle the growing number of free blacks to Africa. The resulting state of Liberia would declare its independence on July 26, 1847, and become the second black republic, after Haiti, in the world.

"The African Americans, with their resources and superior education, set themselves up as the self-appointed leadership, creating tensions with the 16 indigenous tribes of Liberia," explained Mr. Richards. "It was not a sustainable situation," he explained, "The indigenous population demanded their share of power." The present-day situation has its roots in this conflict. In the 1970s the Americo-Liberians, as they came to be known, were pitted against the Liberian Blacks. In the resulting chaos, opportunists on both sides of the conflict flooded in to pillage the country's natural resources.

◆

My rapidly fading hope this July afternoon is that Mrs. Sirleaf will politely accept President Obiang's assurances of commitment to democratic rule and even offer a few words of encouragement, all of it couched in the usual vague diplomacy-speak of the UN.

Here in this nondescript outer office, President Obiang and I have been asked to wait. I can't quite read the president's expression, but I know he is not accustomed to waiting for people to see him. He is, after all, a head of state, a man of power and wealth. I cast a sidelong glance at him. He is smallish of stature, dressed in an impeccably tailored suit. I have difficulty imagining the man behind those thick eyeglasses violently overthrowing his uncle, then having him executed by firing squad.

It is announced that Mrs. Sirleaf will see us now, and we are ushered into her office. She stands to greet us. She is not tall but somehow dominates the office. There is a confidence to her gestures, a grace mixed with something more that I cannot quite define—determination? Pleasantries are exchanged. The mood is formal but polite, even cordial. Mrs. Sirleaf sits in a worn, UN-issued leather armchair, President Obiang on a matching couch. The president opens with greetings from the people of Equatorial Guinea and then begins his prepared remarks. He speaks in Spanish which I translate into English. All the right phrases are in his brief remarks—his government will build democratic institutions, support human rights, encourage opposition political parties to form. He recognizes that the 1996 election was not perfect, but the country is young, the government is learning and it will do better.

Ellen Johnson Sirleaf leans back in her chair, her expression relaxed, her long slender fingers clasped in her lap. She listens intently and nods respectfully throughout the allocution, her eyes studying the face of the powerful man seated opposite her. President Obiang finishes and sits back in his chair. He looks as if he is expecting applause.

Mrs. Sirleaf leans forward, her hands now unfolded and poised to move in gesture. It is time for the President's civics lesson. She speaks in a calm, measured voice, never taking her penetrating gaze from President Obiang's face.

"True democracy," she instructs him, "means transparency and accountability, respect for the rights of all individuals, a free press, the presence of real political opposition and fair elections." Without saying it directly, she dismisses his presidential victory as illegitimate. As I translate into Spanish, President Obiang seems to sink a little deeper into the couch. He has the air of a chastened schoolboy who is being sent home because of poor grades.

All the while, I am captivated by Ellen Johnson Sirleaf. Her quiet, commanding presence, a mix of sureness and authority that she has earned, is striking. She has been tested. She has fought the good fight for democracy in Africa and has suffered the consequences, but she continues the fight. Her words have a moral weight that President Obiang's could never obtain. Then, suddenly, a revelation comes to me so strongly it interrupts my translation. This is the kind of leader that Africa is capable of producing! Can you imagine what the continent would look like if more people like Ellen Johnson Sirleaf were in charge?

I stumble through the remaining phrases, trying to convey their full meaning in Spanish. The president looks increasingly annoyed. But at the moment, I am more concerned about what Mrs. Sirleaf must think of me, thrusting this man in front of her with his little pantomime about democracy in Equatorial Guinea. I feel ashamed, as if somehow I have betrayed her trust, this woman I barely know.

♦

It is later, after President Obiang has climbed into his waiting limousine and returned to his luxury hotel, that I take some time to reflect, not only on how things went today— badly—but on how this job has gone for me these past few years—badly, punctuated by the occasional gem of "pretty good" and even a few times, "exhilarating."

Clearly, with the Obiang experience, my brave declaration of independence and ethical choice in the clients I represent has met reality and lost. There have been major changes at BMS&K. Paul Manafort is out. Despite our regular toe-to-toe confrontations, and even one screaming argument, I miss my former boss. Or to be more precise, I miss knowing what obstacles I had to face and how to work around them. Now I'm adrift, not sure what direction the firm will go in or what my role will be.

I've grown professionally, I remind myself. I've learned a great deal. To shore up my sagging confidence, I try to recall the good experiences where I made the kind of positive difference that I aspired to when I first took this job.

There was my trip to Nicaragua in 1989 as an international observer in the country's first multiparty election which pitted the Sandinistas and Daniel Ortega against the National Opposition Union and their underdog candidate, Violeta Barrios Torres de Chamorro. The consensus opinion held that Ortega was a lock to win, by fair means or foul. But as my fellow observers and I traveled across the lush tropical countryside and met the villagers and farmers and shopkeepers, we could see their hope and enthusiasm for this strange new process called a free election. It was then that I knew that Chamorro had a real chance. If there were enough of us observing the process, the odds were better that the election would be fair and the results would stand. And that is precisely what happened. I felt that I had played my small part on a very large stage.

The adventure was not without its harrowing moments. In the town of El Diario, our SUV suddenly came upon a Sandinista-led funeral cortege of six caskets, presumably young Sandinista soldiers killed by the US-backed Contras. When the crowd spied our car with the sign "Center for Democracy, USA," the funeral turned into a mob. We barely made it out of the town and never checked in at the polling station.

In 1993, I was present in South Africa during the transition period from apartheid to the historic election of Nelson Mandela. Working pro bono as a political party trainer, I invested a lot of myself to build trust with the leaders of the Black Consciousness Movement (BCM). Eventually, after much effort, a number of setbacks, and one passionate exchange where silverware was tossed at me and at my flip chart, I became one of the first outsiders accepted into the BCM inner circle where I made the case for a peaceful transition of power. I added my voice to those who urged the group to step back from its radical sloganeering—"one settler, one bullet"—and to end its threats to disrupt South Africa's first all-race elections. Instead, we pleaded, they should accept the responsibility of governing in a democratic, post-apartheid nation.

Later, as a UN Election Observer, at a remote polling station in Kwa-Zulu-Natal, on April 27, 1994, I witnessed one of the great moments of twentieth-century history as Nelson Mandela was elected president of South Africa. To have been even a small part of that world-changing event was exhilarating, the most satisfying thing I had done in my job and in my life up to that point.

So how did I get here, trying to sell Teodoro Obiang Nguema Mbasogo to Ellen Johnson Sirleaf? On that summer afternoon in New York City in 1996, I have the overwhelming sense of being at a personal crossroads. It is time to stop and examine what I am doing and why. I need to put everything on the table and take a brutally honest look at my life. What difference have I really made? What lasting good have I done?

What would Oma say if she were standing here before me? I wish with all my heart that she were. Would she think that I am adrift? Would she reassure me that all of this is life's journey, that I am accumulating experiences and lessons that will be able to apply with meaning one day? Would she think my trials so trivial, given the decisions she had to grapple with in her lifetime?

I am sure of a few things that I know to be right and good. My husband, Jeff, my infant daughter, Kylie. My unshakeable belief that there are good people in the world dedicated to doing for others, and that I want to be one of them. And this, a new thought that is just beginning to take root and grow: Ellen Johnson Sirleaf will make history. She will change the world. I don't know how she will do it, or what it will entail. But I know that I want to help her. I want to come along on that journey. I want to work for Ellen Johnson Sirleaf.

THREE

THE WARLORD VS.
THE GRANDMOTHER

Northern Virginia
Winter, 1997

Hash browns, rye toast, a chocolate-glazed donut, and a vanilla shake. These are my table companions in this cheerfully nondescript hotel coffee shop in northern Virginia. And frankly, I feel like I could devour the whole spread in a single bite. I am famished. My hunger is fueled by my condition. I am five months pregnant with my second child. Maybe eating will silence the intermittent contractions I have been experiencing since four o'clock this morning. Maybe food will calm my nerves.

I spread out my papers and folders, attempting to occupy the full territory of this four-person booth. Three men and a woman, all sporting white plastic nametags, wait to be seated. They shoot disapproving looks in my direction, but I pretend to ignore them. *Don't mess with me*, I whisper to myself. I am an expectant mother who has managed to get her bloated self to this international conference on economic development in Africa, a virtual *Who's Who* of Americans and Africans doing business in Africa. And in a few minutes, in this very booth, I will meet with one of the featured speakers at this conference, Ellen Johnson Sirleaf. I plan to ask her—if need be, to beg her—to let me work for her. I am convinced that Mrs. Sirleaf is the future of her country, perhaps even the future of Africa.

In the few months since I met her, I have learned more details about her life. She's a 57-year-old mother of four and a grandmother, a Harvard-trained economist with an extensive public service record and a career in international banking. She rose to the position of Minster of Finance in Liberia and introduced reforms to halt financial corruption when the 1980 military coup ultimately forced her into exile. She was twice imprisoned, received multiple death threats and barely escaped the country with her life. Later, she worked for the World Bank in Washington before joining the United Nations.

She has used the platform of the United Nations to argue that Africa must democratize like the rest of the world. "There can be no excuses," she is known to say. She often points out that Apartheid was not the only evil on the continent. Her advocacy of African development is equaled by few others on the world stage.

From everything I know and have read about Mrs. Sirleaf, it is clear that even in exile, her heart and soul are in Liberia. She has remained an outspoken critic of government corruption and the rampant bloodshed in her country. Now she is very likely planning to return home to seek the presidency in what the world hopes will be a fair and democratic election. The only thing standing in her way is her opponent, the murderous warlord Charles Taylor, who has threatened to have her assassinated if she returns to Liberia. It is a dangerous and difficult situation, politically and diplomatically—just the kind of affair that I am really good at getting myself involved in.

My belly tightens like a drum as I feel the grip of another contraction. I take a noisy slurp of my vanilla shake and try not to picture a scenario in which I am carted off to a hospital in the middle of my interview. I look at my watch. This is the second contraction in less than five minutes. Just what my husband Jeff was worried about this morning as I tried on and rejected a half-dozen outfits, creating a mounting pile on our bed. I settled on a white blouse and black jumper, black tights and boots. I stared at myself in the mirror. "You look like a penguin," I muttered.

"Should I call Dr. Newman?" Jeff asked cautiously.

"No, I'm fine."

"Are you sure?"

"Yes, I'm sure!" I replied testily, looking at myself disapprovingly in the mirror and wondering how I was going to keep my confidence for the day.

"Riva?"

"What do you want?" I snapped.

"Here's your shawl," he replied calmly, before retreating to a safer part of the house.

"Thank you," I called out cheerily, probably confirming Jeff's concerns about my mental as well as my physical state.

Here in the crowded coffee shop, I take long, slow breaths and try to rearrange my shawl to cover my belly. I don't want to give Mrs. Sirleaf any reason to reject me. Sure, I may be out of circulation for a while with a newborn. But only a short while, I reassure myself. I'll be back up and running in no time, I insist, rehearsing my lines. I reflect that I am facing yet again the primary tension in my job: needing to work for the clients who pay while being drawn to the clients who inspire. I know Mrs. Sirleaf has limited resources right now, relying on her personal savings rather than large donors or government backing. But that only makes her more appealing. To me, she epitomizes the caliber of leadership available to Africans if only they can break free of fear and corruption and see the opportunity that people like Ellen Johnson Sirleaf represent.

I look up to see her striding confidently toward me. She is awash in color, dressed in a blue, black and yellow African dress of exquisite design, with matching head covering and a swatch of bright, contrasting green cloth thrown over her left shoulder. Glancing down at myself, I feel again like a penguin—a bloated one—facing a luminous cockatoo. Her furrowed brow, deep frown and pensive eyes makes her seem somewhat stern and unapproachable. I am relieved that she doesn't seem to notice my protruding belly as we shake hands.

"Mrs. Sirleaf," I begin, "it's a pleasure to see you again."

"Call me Ellen. Yes, I remember our first meeting," she says, with a hint of disapproval. "Are you still working with President Obiang?"

I feel my face flush. "I am."

"Do you believe he is standing by his commitment to democracy and good governance?" she asks, leveling her gaze squarely at mine. Normally, this is the moment in my job where I deliver my prepared talking points: Oh, yes. The Obiang government is now implementing important democratic reforms on multiple levels throughout the country.

"No," I say flatly. I am not here to bullshit this woman I so admire.

Ellen nods solemnly but maintains her stern countenance. She invites me to sit. It's time to get to the business at hand. I sit awkwardly. If only my shawl were the size of a blanket, I think.

Ellen leans forward and clasps her hands together. "I fear the July election in Liberia will have the same outcome for Charles Taylor as it did for President Obiang in his election last February," she states. My face heats up again. My belly flips. There is a challenge in her words, as if she is expecting me to offer a rebuttal. "Obiang won with 98 percent of the vote. Wasn't that it?" she asks.

"Yes," I admit.

Ellen moves on, thankfully.

"Taylor will make sure he wins, either through a flawed election or the continuation of mass murder."

I fumble for what to say. "Are the odds that heavily in his favor?"

"Of course!" she says with irritation, and I fear that my question sounded naïve.

"He is the frontrunner because he has stolen the country's resources to back his campaign. He is using bribery to lure voters into his camp, and bloodshed and intimidation to cow the rest. A Liberia under Charles Taylor would be one in which human and individual rights would continue to be rendered completely meaningless."

Of course I know that she is right. I have done my homework on Taylor. His quest for control of Liberia began back in 1985 when he escaped from a maximum-security state correctional facility in Plymouth, Massachusetts. He was being held, pending deportation hearings, on charges of embezzling nearly $1 million in funds from the Liberian government. There were rumors that the CIA had a hand in engineering Taylor's escape. In 1989, he surfaced in Liberia with a band of guerrillas, financed, armed and trained by Libyan leader Muammar Gaddafi. He attempted to depose President and Master Sergeant Samuel Doe, the first indigenous Liberian leader who came to power in a bloody coup d'état, and after ten years of rule, had grown increasingly corrupt, intolerant, and some would say sociopathic.

The fight for Monrovia between rival warlords was brutal and indiscriminate. The civilian population that did not flee on foot remained trapped in their tin, wood, or cardboard homes with no access to food, water or medicine. US Marines were called in to evacuate thousands of American embassy staff, US citizens and citizens of other nationalities. It would be one of many evacuations over the course of the next decade. Doe was eventually assassinated by the forces of rival warlord, Prince Johnson. He was grossly tortured, both his ears chopped off, his manhood too—a spectacle shown on state television. A civil war erupted, with Taylor battling Prince Johnson and other warlords for control of post-Doe Liberia.

Ellen initially indicated her support for Taylor's military campaign, believing that Doe was a monster—she herself was twice victimized—and that all efforts had to be sought for his removal. But after witnessing Taylor's actions, the senseless killings, the ruthless quest for power, she became his most vocal critic.

Her earlier support of Taylor haunts Ellen to this day.

The war would go on for six years until Taylor's faction gained control over much of the country and its resources. Finally, in 1996, a West African Peace Keeping Force comprised mostly of Nigerians, brokered a ceasefire. National elections were scheduled for July 1997.

"More than 150,000 people have died since the war began," Ellen states grimly, "and more than half the population has been displaced or forced into exile." Among the many atrocities, Taylor's troops forcibly drafted hundreds of young boys into a violent squad known as the Small Boys Unit. There were reports that the boys were kept addicted to drugs. They would venture into villages, hand out candy and lollipops, then pull out their guns and fire at innocent people. It was a systematic reign of terror.

Ellen's voice deepens as her outrage increases. "Sexual violence, child soldiers—a complete breakdown in the structures that define Liberian society." She clenches her fist. "He must be stopped." Now with her country still in Taylor's grip, this woman sitting across from me is about to toss her hat into the ring and run for president.

"Have you declared your candidacy?" I ask, trying to mask the next contraction that takes my breath away.

"Not yet," she replies. "But there is so little time. I would prefer it if the election were postponed. However, the international community, including the UN, won't have it. They want the Nigerian peacekeepers out of Liberia."

"I know this is true for the US administration," I add. "The peacekeeping force is costly. The Americans want to cross Liberia off their agenda."

Ellen nods in acknowledgement. "I can either stand on the sidelines and throw stones or jump in and see if I can impact the process. This is where I need someone to help, here in this country. I must make certain that the United States is paying attention." She pauses, and for an instant I can feel the immense weight of her decision. "I must provide Liberians an alternative to Taylor," she declares.

I attempt to take a deep breath. This is the moment for my pitch.

"Ellen, if anyone can make the US pay attention, it's me. I have the contacts and I know how the game works. You have a compelling message and that's the most important element in mobilizing support in Washington. We'll need to rely on Congress to challenge the administration's apathy. But since the administration is Democrat and the Congress is Republican, that shouldn't be too hard."

Boom, another contraction hits. *Shit. They're marching steadily through me now every few minutes.*

"Ellen, I'm pregnant," I blurt out. "I'm due in early May. I have a whole team of colleagues to support me, and I'll still be directing our US efforts. But if my having a baby right now is a problem for you, I'll understand."

Suddenly Ellen smiles. It is so bright and ebullient that it seems to lift her small five-foot, six-inch frame right out of her chair.

"It is a nice shawl, Riva, but it disguises very little. Congratulations. Of course, having a baby is not a problem."

"I'm good then?" I ask.

"You are good," Ellen replies. But now she quickly shifts back to business. "I know I will need to raise my profile for this campaign. Taylor is the main competitor. He is waging a campaign of fear. But I want to portray just the opposite—compassion."

I jump right in. "How about we position the campaign as 'The Warlord vs. the Grandmother'? That will emphasize the contrast."

"I like it!" She claps her hands, punctuating her words.

"We have only three months and limited resources," I continue. "Your core constituency is women. It is their sons, grandsons, brothers and husbands who have been killed—or have become killers."

"Yes," Ellen agrees solemnly. "It is Liberia's women who have carried the burden of this war. But with Taylor's threat of continued bloodshed, will they dare to vote? Will they feel they have a free choice?"

"That will be part of *my* job," I respond. "If you can show momentum and we can convince Liberians that you have strong backing from the US and other powerful nations, then we've got a chance. Maybe then those women will vote for a better future."

"Instead of voting their fear," Ellen adds solemnly. She stands and I too get awkwardly to my feet. She holds out her hand. "We have a deal," she says. And that luminous smile returns.

◆

An hour later, I am flat on my back at Columbia Women's Hospital in Washington, DC, an I.V. in my arm, a fetal monitor strapped to my belly and a frowning Dr. Newman standing over me.

"Braxton-Hicks," he declares. "Very common. Not usually a problem. But yours are too regular. You're only five months and two weeks. I'm very concerned."

He gives me that paternal, disapproving look. "I'm your doctor. I need you to hear me."

"Okay, shoot," I reply, trying to appear as if I am in control and totally at ease.

"To stop the onset of labor, you need to rest, reduce the stress in your life, and take Terbutaline every four hours for the next two months. Are you listening to me?"

I am and I'm not. "The medication," I reply, "fine. The other two, highly unlikely."

"What am I going to do with you?" asks the good doctor. I smile at him reassuringly.

Two days later, I dutifully take a morning to rest and compose my memo to Ellen, outlining a two-part plan of action. Plan A will be to compel the international community to stop Charles Taylor, a convicted criminal, from becoming leader of Liberia. Taylor's victory will destabilize the sub-region. He has plundered Liberia's natural resources. He should be forbidden to use these same resources to finance his campaign.

To be honest, I'm not optimistic that Plan A will work. It is clear that the international community—including the Clinton Administration—will not block Taylor's candidacy. They want a free, democratic election to take place, even if only in appearance. The broader concern isn't Liberia's election, but getting the Nigerian peacekeeping forces back to their own country. The forces are undisciplined and corrupt, and they empower an unelected Nigerian general to take a regional leadership role. That general is former Nigerian Defense Minister Sani Abacha, who quickly dissolved all democratic institutions in Nigeria and replaced elected governors with military officials. He has a well-earned reputation for corruption.

Still, it's worth a try.

Plan B will be to ensure that the United States, the United Nations and other stakeholders guarantee that a sufficient number of election observers are present on voting day to make certain that the election is free and fair—or as free and fair as possible. We will insist that specific benchmarks be met. If they aren't, we will press for a postponement.

With this strategy in place, it is official. I am representing Ellen Johnson Sirleaf, candidate for president of Liberia.

◆

Home from work later that week, I am heating up frozen lasagna for dinner when the phone rings. "Hi Riva, this is Jennie, Ellen's older sister from New York."

Wondering how she got my home number only two days after I signed my agreement with Ellen, I answer, "So the word is out."

Jennie laughs. "You will find we are a small community."

"What can I do for you?" I ask.

"Riva," she says, sounding like she's known me her whole life, "we do not believe Ellen should run for president. Taylor has promised to kill her if she returns to Liberia. Besides, she is spending her retirement on this campaign. She will have nothing left for the future."

"Jennie, this is something that Ellen needs to do. Neither you nor I can change her mind. You know that."

"We are very worried about her," Jennie replies.

"I understand. I'm doing everything I can to ensure that the US Embassy makes it clear to Taylor that if anything happens to Ellen, he will be held responsible. We're going to make her return to Monrovia a very high profile, public event. With the international media covering her campaign, there'll be less chance for any incidents."

Jennie voice falters. "We must all do our best to protect her, and we must pray."

"Absolutely," I reassure her.

"Oh!" Jennie blurts. "Congratulations! I hear you're expecting!"

Wow, I think, word does get out fast in this family.

"Thank you. It's my second."

"Bless your heart. How are those contractions?"

I laugh. "Better, thank you. And Jennie, my line is open to you and your family any time."

From then on, the phone calls never stop. I become an unofficial Liberian and a member of Ellen's close-knit family.

On Saturday, April 12, despite continued death threats, Ellen boards a flight from Abidjan to Monrovia to return home after her years in exile.

She is anticipating her nomination as the presidential candidate of the Liberian Action Party (LAP). All had been decided a long time ago. Her association with LAP was in fact what landed her in prison. Ellen was its founding member, its spiritual leader.

But while she is in transit, there is a change of heart. The LAP holds an emergency convention and nominates Cletus Wotorson as its standard bearer, withdrawing its support for Ellen. Ellen had prepared for the assaults of Charles Taylor, but the disloyalty of her own party takes her by surprise. It will not be the last time that the Liberian political establishment turns on her.

Even so, Ellen lets nothing get in the way of her emotional return home from exile. "It must be a joyous occasion," says Ellen.

As I promised Jennie, the US ambassador is present to meet Ellen upon arrival. Central Monrovia swarms with supporters welcoming her home, their very own "Iron Lady," the nickname she received in the late 1980s after she was released from prison the second time.

I wait for Ellen's call the day she arrives. I know it is Ellen when I pick up the phone and hear horrible static on the line.

"You should see the crowd!" she exclaims. "There were thousands of Liberians—young, old, women, and men! I am home, Riva, where I belong!" Before I can share in her enthusiasm, her tone shifts abruptly. "What have you accomplished from your side?"

"What do you mean?" I ask, a bit deflated. "The US ambassador was there to greet you. *The New York Times* reporter was on your plane to cover your return."

"I know, but what else?" she presses.

I learn quickly that I am not allowed to rest on my laurels with Ellen. No one is.

Ellen quickly regroups with her supporters. On April 18, barely one week later, she accepts the nomination of the Unity Party (UP). At a rally in Monrovia's City Hall, she proclaims her loyalty to her new party followers and states that "one of the greatest tasks ahead will be the reconstruction of the war-time economy."

Throughout April, Ellen continues to draw huge crowds everywhere she goes. Returning from a rally in Nimba County, Ellen is euphoric. "There were tens of thousands of people today at the rally!" she exclaims. "We're doing it, Riva, we're capturing the imagination of the people."

My job is not to be a cheerleader, but to stay focused on the task at hand. "That's great," I reply, "but do you know how many of them are registered voters?"

"Not offhand," she answers. "The campaign manager will have those details."

"What's the plan to ensure that all those people at the rally actually vote for you?"

"Someone else is taking care of that," she admonishes.

The static on the line and in our conversation distracts us both.

"You have to stress with your team that it's the turnout on Election Day that really matters," I remind her. "Not the cheering crowds."

I repeat the same drill each time we speak, but I never get a straight answer from Ellen or her advisors. And that bothers me.

A few weeks pass and I grow huge. I am convinced the drugs that I am taking are creating a monster baby because none of my maternity clothes fit, even though my due date is still weeks away. My colleagues in DC are increasingly nervous when I make the rounds. No one wants me to deliver on the office floor. I dedicate my time to preparing Ellen's campaign literature from home—the "Only Ellen" platform, a 26-page packet making the case that because of her history in the struggle and her competency, only she, *Only Ellen* as the Unity Party candidate, can take the country from tyranny to democracy in 1997. "Efficiency, honesty and rule of law will be the bedrocks of her administration," it says in bold on the first page.

Our efforts are paying off. By the end of April, Ellen is gaining momentum in the polls. An independent survey published in *The Liberian Daily Observer* sampled more than 18,000 potential voters and placed Ellen in the lead over the other candidates with 25 percent of the vote. I am suspicious of the sampling, but Ellen's campaign team is elated.

On Friday, May 2, still more than a week from my due date, my doctor takes a measurement of my belly and announces the news. "Riva, we need to induce you this weekend. If this baby gets any bigger, with your small frame, you won't be able to deliver."

"Can we please wait until Monday?" I ask. I want to spend the weekend with my daughter Kylie and finish Ellen's campaign materials. Luckily, my son Andrew cooperates with my plan. He is born on May 6 and weighs in at nearly nine pounds. He is so big they have to deliver him one shoulder at a time. I receive dozens of phone calls from my newly adopted Liberian family.

All of our hopes, those of my growing family, American and Liberian, are that on Election Day in Liberia, just two months away, Ellen Johnson Sirleaf will shock her country, the continent and the world by beating the warlord Charles Taylor in a free election. It will be a heroic, historic triumph, the African story of the year. We all know we still have an uphill battle. The question is: Just how high is that hill?

Ellen Johnson Sirleaf and VP running mate, Peter K. Bemah, Monrovia, April 1997.

FOUR

LIVE TO FIGHT ANOTHER DAY

Falls Church, Virginia
June, 1997

By mid-June Ellen Johnson Sirleaf's popularity is soaring. In the towns of Kakata, Harbel and Smell No Taste, Ellen the presidential candidate is greeted by cheering crowds wearing the green and white campaign colors of her Unity Party. Something truly remarkable is happening. It appears that Ellen has tapped into a national feeling of hope and desire for change in a country that has suffered so many years of armed conflict. There seems to be a growing confidence among the people, many of them women, that they will finally be allowed to vote in a free election for the candidate of their choice. It is all shaping up as the continent's most inspiring story and the rest of the world is starting to pay attention. "Ellen Johnson Sirleaf to lead new alliance capable of taking forces to victory" (*The Inquirer*). "New alliance unfolds, Sirleaf gets more support" (*The Observer*). "Woman in tight race to lead Liberia, ex UN official and warlord neck-and-neck" *(The Washington Times)*. Can the grandmother really beat the warlord? That was the question on the Liberian street, and well beyond.

And the answer is: Not if warlord-turned-candidate Charles Taylor can help it.

Taylor's idea of an election campaign is to use his gang of armed thieves to threaten voters and terrorize Ellen's campaign workers and volunteers. One graphic example is Napolean Zoegar, a middle-aged truck driver and father from Sanniquelle. He is beaten so badly that he almost loses his sight, his green and white T-shirt ripped off of his body and pounded with excrement.

With each day that passes, the risk to Ellen grows. Liberia is inundated with weapons—the remnants of a decade of civil conflict. In contrast to Ellen's volunteers, Taylor's campaign team consists of war-hardened militia, who coerce voters using combat tactics: roadblocks, physical threats and intimidation. The only saving grace for Ellen so far is that the world is watching through international media and third-country election observers. To maintain appearances, Taylor presents the signs of an actual political contest with his expensive, glossy posters affixed everywhere throughout Monrovia. But as with most things in the time of Taylor, they are not what they appear to be. The posters are used to mark territory, like a male dog urinating. As for Ellen's posters, the few that appear are torn down within hours.

Unregulated weapons are not the only obstacles that stand between Ellen and her goal of the presidency. Her pension funds, the principle source of her campaign financing, are dwindling fast. Taylor, meanwhile, has an overflowing campaign chest amassed from his ongoing illegal exploitation of the country's natural resources—gold, timber and diamonds. It is a criminal enterprise he will soon export to neighboring Sierra Leone, with tragic results.

Ellen's campaign trail outside the capital has to be navigated with the rusted, worn out, rented vehicles, typically lacking windows and stripped of their side-view mirrors. Several times she fails to make it to a scheduled campaign appearance because her driver exhausts his spare tires on Liberia's cratered roads. Taylor, however, has imported a fleet of brand new, cream-colored minibuses from China and an eight-seat helicopter from neighboring Côte d'Ivoire. He has sole access to the heavily forested and inaccessible parts of the countryside as well as the singular ability to transport voters to the polls. His convoy sheds bags of rice to Liberians along the way, promising, "There will be more rewards for all who vote for Charles Taylor."

With few resources, Ellen is highly dependent on volunteer grassroots supporters. She clings to her hope and prayer that the Liberian people, despite it all, will exercise their free will. Surely they will choose her, she reasons.

By month's end, sixteen political parties narrow to six, with almost all opposition parties backing Ellen. Liberian news organizations, those not controlled by Taylor, place Ellen and Taylor neck-and-neck and call her the "People's candidate." As a result, we all believe that Ellen is doing the impossible: gradually surmounting Taylor's vast advantages. During the second week of June, however, disturbing reports begin to come in from the greater Montserrado region. In Liberia's outlying counties like Nimba, Bong, and Lofa, Taylor is in firm control. These areas are so dangerous that no other candidates can safely campaign there. Taylor runs the local radio stations, which he uses as a tool of mob mobilization every time a "traitor" enters his stronghold. His followers threaten villagers, and they leave their "examples," like Napolean from Sanniquelle, making his campaign of fear truly palpable.

♦

It is a hot and hazy first of July day in Falls Church, Virginia, and while my two month-old son Andrew has been napping (thankfully), I have been dialing and redialing Ellen's cell number. The phone is our lifeline, and often I have to wait hours for a call to go through.

There is nothing to fuel postpartum irritability like the jarring sound of a failed international call blasting your ear. That's why I practically fall out of my chair when my phone rings and the static on the line lets me know that it is Ellen. The connection is worse than ever.

What I hear is "… slogan… kill me… postpone…"

"Ellen," I say, "please speak up and talk slowly."

Please, God, give us a break, I pray. This is so important. I can tell by the tremor in Ellen's voice that she is beyond agitated.

"Do you know what Taylor's campaign slogan is now? 'He killed my Ma, he killed my Pa. I will vote for him, or he will kill me'!" Amid the static, I reflect in amazement that Taylor is rewriting the rules of dirty campaigning.

"We must try to postpone the election," Ellen continues urgently. "All of the other parties are signing a petition. It will mean nothing without US support."

"I'm on it, Ellen," I reply as the static overwhelms the connection and the call is lost. But the message is clear. We move now to our Plan B. Somehow we have to convince this administration and the United States government that the playing field in Liberia has become drastically uneven and corrupt. In the interests of democracy and the future of the country, the elections in Liberia need to be postponed, now. This is not going to be an easy sell, but that has rarely stopped me before. And this time, there are lives at stake, including the life of the woman I admire and have pledged to help.

I draft an Action Memo under Ellen's signature and align it with the Liberian opposition parties. I rush to distribute it to the major players—the US State Department, the National Security Council, the Foreign Affairs Committees in Congress, and the international organizations slated to observe next month's election. I have to be political in my arguments. I can't say directly to State Department officials, for example, that Taylor is a murdering, blood-thirsty embezzler and thug who is terrorizing Liberians so he can steal the presidential election. No, I have to be more circumspect. I have to make my case—our case—with non-polemic, diplomatic ease.

And so I add the proper phrases: "…fundamental electoral issues have yet to be adequately addressed in Liberia. This includes the development of voter education and registration programs, the repatriation of Liberian refugees—numbered in the hundreds of thousands—who wish to participate in the election, the preparation of materials, such as voter identification cards and ballots, the training of domestic election observers to complement the international observers…"

I add my warning which is also Ellen's plea: "Unless each of these areas receives the careful and immediate attention it deserves and can be resolved before the election takes place on July 19, there is little hope that the upcoming process will be free and fair. There is even less hope that Liberians will have any chance at the democracy they deserve."

I close the memo by quoting Kevin George, the president of Friends of Liberia, a private voluntary organization started in 1986 by returning Peace Corps Volunteers. In his testimony before Congress in June, Kevin stated, "The US government should reiterate that the date for the election, while important, is not as important as verifying that the conditions for free and fair elections are in place."

My first stop is to see Ed Royce, Republican of California, Chairman of the Africa Subcommittee of the US House of Representatives. Royce is one of the few members of Congress, outside of the Congressional Black Caucus, who truly understands and cares deeply about Africa. Royce is also a powerful Republican committee chairman who is highly critical of the Clinton administration's foreign policy.

Royce was one of the first US officials (Administration or Congress) to be convinced of what a Taylor victory could mean for Liberia and the stability of the sub-region. Royce suggests that a congressional letter be prepared, which can then be made public to draw attention to the flaws in the upcoming Liberian election. "It will be a single step," we are told, but neither he nor I nor any of his staff are optimistic that a single congressional action will change the momentum of a Taylor victory. But not acting is not an option.

On July 10 a letter is sent to the Honorable Henry Andrews, chairman of the Independent Elections Commission of Liberia. It is signed by a dozen members of the Foreign Affairs Committee with the hope that a direct appeal from the US Congress can have impact. The letter states, "We are concerned about Liberia's readiness for Presidential and Legislative Elections, particularly in light of the sentiment in favor of a postponement recently expressed by 12 of the 13 parties vying for elected office."

The Congressional initiative is helpful, but by itself hardly sufficient. The biggest hurdle still awaits us—the US State Department and the institutional wariness of all things African, especially after the spectacular policy failures in Somalia and Rwanda. We find ourselves with a very big boulder to push up a very steep hill.

♦

With the Congressional letter already published on the wires and a copy in hand, I clear through security at the State Department's C Street entrance for my meeting with Howard Jeter, the special envoy to Liberia.

Jeter reports to the Assistant Secretary of State for African Affairs, Susan E. Rice. At the time, Rice was the youngest-ever to hold the position, appointed by President Clinton in 1997 at the age of 33. Prior to that she served as Clinton's senior advisor for African Affairs. Later she would go on to become President Obama's foreign policy advisor during his 2008 campaign, his UN Ambassador and then his National Security advisor. Lamentably, I never found myself on the same side of any issue with Susan Rice.

On my way to the African Bureau, I am directed by my escort to "just go down the hallway until you can't go no further." The hallway is an obstacle course of old furniture, scaffolding, paint tarps, and stray carpentry nails. Most of the fluorescent, overhead lights buzz or blink or remain dark. This State Department corridor feels like the developing world, especially because there's not a carpenter or construction worker in sight. I hope that this isn't a reflection of the State Department's commitment to African affairs, with Liberia relegated to the category of Siberia: out of sight, out of mind.

Through an open door at the end of the hallway I see a man at a desk. The scene strikes me as slightly bizarre for this highly proper place. He is a prominent African American diplomat with salt-and-pepper hair and a distinguished air about him, sitting there in a black suit. But there is no receptionist or a sign indicating his name and title. He looks up from his neat and tidy desk as I approach and smiles in the way that indicates a) he is not happy to see me; b) what I have to say is a waste of time; or, c) both.

I take a seat and notice that there are no personal touches—no family photos, framed diplomas, no plants in need of sun and water. I am aware that this post is a stepping-stone for Mr. Jeter, as he will soon be named the new ambassador to Nigeria.

"Please have a seat, Riva," he says politely.

But don't get too comfortable, I think. He knows that I am not on the same page as the administration, and my work with Congress on behalf of Ellen is viewed as muckraking at best, and irritating for sure.

"Mr. Ambassador," I begin, "I'm here because Ellen Johnson Sirleaf reports to me that there is no freedom to campaign. Taylor's militia controls the countryside. There's no access to media, because Taylor controls the only radio station that reaches the entire country. She doesn't believe the playing field is level and the opposition parties need more time to challenge him. All of the political parties," I stress, "save for Taylor's, are asking for a postponement of the elections."

He smiles. Here it comes.

"I understand her concerns," he replies, "but we cannot expect a perfect election after a decade of civil war. We cannot let perfection be the enemy of the good."

Perfection is the enemy of the good? Did I miss that motivational poster on my way down the hallway?

"But it's a campaign of fear," I reply. "Taylor is saying that if he doesn't win, the war will continue. Have you heard his campaign slogan?"

Jeter nods, assuming a solemn expression.

My frustration grows, and I lean forward, ready to do whatever it takes to get him to listen. "Ellen warns that if Taylor is legitimized through a flawed election, he will be a cancer for the entire sub-region— Sierra Leone, Guinea, Côte d'Ivoire. It won't be only the people of Liberia who will suffer."

Jeter rubs his palms together, assuming a thoughtful posture. "We have to respect the free will of the Liberian people. If they choose Taylor, we must respect that choice."

"I'm suggesting to you, sir, that the Liberian people don't have a free will or a choice in this election."

Without a hesitation, he says, "We believe that this election is a good first step in that direction."

These are the moments in which diplomacy feels far too close to getting a root canal. I want to scream. Break something. Flail my arms and shout. Instead I take a deep breath. "How can the US possibly continue to support this process?"

He gazes at me calmly, but no words leave his mouth. Apparently he thinks my question is rhetorical. It is not.

"Why can't the United States play a leadership role in calling for a postponement," I ask, "so that the opposition parties can be given a fair chance?" I am practically pleading with him now. "In your testimony to Congress on June 24, didn't you state that if the US perceives it is not possible to conduct a free and fair election, then it will use diplomatic and other means to address the failures in the process?"

"Yes, I did," acknowledges Jeter. He pauses. "Riva, as Ellen knows, the election has already been postponed once."

But it is not Jeter's decision. I know that. He is a career Foreign Service Officer, operating with the information he has been provided, and within the political space afforded to him. The Clinton Administration just wants to check Liberia off its "to do" list. I can feel this reality as I wait for the ambassador to respond.

"We believe in the policy of redemption when it comes to Charles Taylor," he finally states.

"Excuse me?" I am so stunned my jaw literally drops.

Jeter places his palms flat on his desk. "It is our view that if Mr. Taylor wins the election, we will recognize him as the president and hope he lives up to his new responsibilities."

Is there a word for "beyond absurd"? I glance at his mostly empty bookshelf, looking for a thesaurus. I cannot believe that a US government official has just said this to me. Mr. Taylor, as this man calls him, who is responsible for the execution of the former Liberian president and the deaths of more than 150,000 innocent civilians—and we believe in the policy of redemption?

"Would you have done the same with Hitler or Stalin?" I ask.

This is not a rhetorical question. I want an answer. I don't get one. Jeter rises and indicates that the meeting is over. As I follow the trail of strewn nails back down the hall, I call Ellen on my cell phone to tell her the news. The Americans have already written her off.

Her response reveals her steadfast nature. "Then we will play the cards we have been dealt," she says. "We need at least to ensure that all observers are in place on Election Day."

◆

When the call ends, I am left with nagging worries and a painful memory. I have seen what can happen when a first-time national election in an African country goes forward without the proper preparation. I have witnessed the chaos that can follow when the international stakeholders are ready to check the box, pack up and go home—when an election is just the continuation of war by other means. I was in Angola in 1992.

On the morning of September 28, polling places across Angola opened promptly at 7:00. Angolans who had never voted before queued for hours to cast their ballots. They carried with them their very first government-issued identification cards. After voting, they proudly displayed their forefingers marked with blue indelible ink. Pictures of smiling Angolans, lined up peacefully to vote, covered the front pages of the world's press. Everything appeared to be running smoothly.

Less than two years earlier, Angola's ruling party, the MPLA (Popular Movement for the Liberation of Angola) had permitted the establishment of a multiparty system. It discarded its Marxist-Leninist ideology and gave a vote of confidence to President Jose Eduardo dos Santos, allowing him to continue peace talks with the National Union for the Total Independence of Angola (UNITA), leading ultimately to what were intended as the country's first free and fair elections. UNITA, led by Dr. Jonas Savimbi, had the support of the apartheid government of South Africa, a serious handicap that made the group anathema to most of black Africa. UNITA had recently received the assistance of the Republican administration under its Freedom Fighter doctrine. My firm had helped secure that assistance. By the time of elections in 1992, my firm had already worked with UNITA for almost five years.

These elections, the world press reported, were to be a milestone, the first material proof of the new détente between the United States and the former Soviet Union, which had long played a role in Angola. The Reagan Administration was convinced that the elections would confirm to all the world that communist ideology cannot survive when people are given an opportunity to express their free will. It was hoped that UNITA, despite the disgrace of accepting support from the apartheid government of South Africa, could now be legitimized through an open electoral process.

By October 1 the results were being reported in from the urban areas where MPLA support was strongest—and reported in very quickly. Tallies from the rural areas known to be loyal to UNITA were not yet available. The MPLA appeared to be winning the election by a landslide. Only 17 election helicopters had been deployed to collect the votes in a country twice the size of Texas in which 70 percent of the population is rural. What was the UN thinking, we wondered? By the time we figured out why the vote count was so distorted, tensions were already at the boiling point. UNITA leaders immediately began to cry foul. There had to be fraud. The communists could not possibly win this election fairly.

By the end of the second day of counting, the MPLA's margin of victory appeared insurmountable. UNITA leaders promised to await the official posting of results, but in reality all their cadres went underground, fearing MPLA reprisal attacks. The only person left standing for UNITA, ready to engage the journalists, the diplomats, the observers, and anyone else who asked, was UNITA's single US representative: me. Manafort did not come, nor did he send any of the other senior BMS&K partners.

After consultation with some of the US election observers, I came up with a plan. I would petition the National Electoral Commission (NEC) to recognize and publicly announce that there were legitimate electoral concerns and to delay the announcement of the winner. It would buy time to allow the votes from the rural areas to come in and then, hopefully, get UNITA back to the table and try to sort out the election anomalies.

I arrived at NEC headquarters without incident. After two hours in an unventilated waiting room, a NEC official finally ushered me into the office of the director, one Luis Barbao, a former official in the Portuguese government who obviously had drawn the short stick to end up with this job. Barbao was about 50, smallish, with salt-and-pepper hair matted to his head. He looked like he hadn't slept in days.

"What would you have me do?" he asked bluntly.

"There are serious claims of fraud," I replied. "The rural vote was underreported. This throws the whole legitimacy of the election into question. You have to delay your formal announcement of the winner until we know that all the remote villages and rural counties have reported and all the votes have been counted."

Barbao rubbed his chin, lit what I presumed was his fiftieth consecutive cigarette of the day, and agreed that he would take the matter under "advisement."

I left the NEC offices at sundown, hopeful that Barbao would take action. I did not see an alternative. My driver pulled up in an orange VW bus and slid open the side door when gun shots erupted in the streets around me. It was a staccato of automatic gunfire and it was close by. My driver panicked and took off without me. Frantic, I looked for somewhere to take cover and dove under a U.N. all-terrain vehicle and waited... and waited... and waited... until finally the gun bursts subsided. For many minutes afterwards I was in shock. My mind could not take in what had happened and my body was shaking uncontrollably. Finally, once the VW bus reappeared, I crawled from my sheltering place. I went directly to the US mission and reported what happened. I told them that I believed it to be a deliberate act of intimidation. By the looks of me, it obviously worked.

After what the US Mission in Angola now called "the incident," I was advised to leave the country. With the help of my Angolan friends, I managed to get a seat on a Sabena commercial flight to Brussels. A couple of weeks later, war broke out in the capital city. Several thousand people, mostly UNITA members and supporters, were slaughtered, including men and women I had known and worked with. The memory is still raw. So yes, there is a price to be paid if an election goes wrong. I did not want to see a repeat tragedy in Liberia.

◆

Undeterred by the obstacles and bolstered by the hope that the many constituents who are crowding her rallies across Liberia will vote for her, Ellen continues to campaign hard. However, on the other side of hope are the facts. American and South African intelligence reports indicate that Taylor will win the first round against all the opposition parties, and will do so with more than 50 percent of the vote.

On Election Day, there are hundreds of international observers in the country and even one former US president. Jimmy Carter is leading the American delegation. Typically, election observers are a blessing. Their presence assures people that their votes will be counted, that intimidation and irregularities will be marked and corrected. In Liberia, though, the observers are a curse. They give legitimacy to an election that is not only terribly flawed, but stolen outright. Taylor wins by upwards of 75 percent of the vote—a percentage recorded at the very first polling station in downtown Monrovia and carried consistently until the official certification by Chairman Andrews of the Independent Elections Commission of Liberia. If this were a free and fair election, this figure would be seen for the fraud that it is.

I am sickened when I hear the news. I remember that February day when I interviewed with Ellen, my shawl camouflaging my protruding belly. She had predicted this outcome: "I fear that the July election will have the same outcome for Taylor that it did for Teodoro Obiang in Equatorial Guinea." Just twenty-four hours after the election, the international observer delegation is set to hold a press conference during which Jimmy Carter will certify the election results. My bitter disappointment is multiplied by absolute frustration at being unable to get through to Ellen despite endless attempts.

My phone is set on repeat dial when a BBC report comes across my office desk. It details a public confrontation between Jimmy Carter and Ellen. Carter is quoted as saying, "I urge Mrs. Johnson Sirleaf to accept these legitimate results and to work with Charles Taylor to rebuild the nation in the spirit of national reconciliation." Ellen's quoted response is to the point, to say the least. "These elections are fraudulent. I will not accept the results. I will not work with a murderer."

Shit. From bad to worse. I don't like it, but I know that I have to intervene. It takes two more hours before I finally reach Ellen. The emotion in her voice is a combination of fury, loss, disappointment, and despondence.

"These elections were stolen!" she shouts into the phone. "It is not possible that of those tens of thousands of people who came to my rallies, only nine percent voted for me! I will not accept the results. None of us will. I told Jimmy Carter this!"

I struggle to remain calm, for I feel almost as strongly as Ellen does. "Ellen, I know what you said to Jimmy Carter. It's all over the world."

Ellen is silent. I continue, summoning an authority I did not know that I could express to this woman. "The election is over. The US, the UN, the European Union, and the African Union will certify the results tomorrow. There's nothing more we can do. If you stand in the way, you'll be labeled as an obstructionist."

"No! I refuse to reconcile with Taylor," she insists.

"You don't have to. But Ellen, listen to me, please. You have to call Jimmy Carter back and let him know that you won't stand in the way of the international certification of the results." She starts to protest, but I forge ahead. "You need to complete this process with your reputation intact." I crumple up the BBC report and toss it into the trash. I picture Ellen in Monrovia, this proud determined woman having to endure the wild celebrations of Charles Taylor's victorious supporters. My heart is breaking for her.

"Ellen, you need to live to fight another day."

There is a long, static-filled pause on the line. At first I think we've lost the connection—or she has hung up on me. Then I hear Ellen's weary voice. Beneath the pain she feels at having failed her country, her supporters, and herself, I can still hear the resolve. She has lost the battle. The war is not over yet.

"You are right, Riva. I will call Mr. Carter."

Two months later, after reality set in and our emotions settled down, we could see more clearly that it would have been impossible to defeat Taylor with the circumstances as they were. Taylor had the name recognition, he had the means, and he had the fear factor.

Ellen reflected, "The Liberians, and the Americans, too, believed that if Taylor didn't win there would be no peace."

Harry Greaves, Ellen's political advisor, remarked, "It was a short-sighted and gross miscalculation of the man and his motivations."

FIVE

MASQUERADING AS A LEGITIMATE STATE

Washington, DC, 1998

It is tough to lose. But it is even tougher when the winner is everything that you fear and worse—a criminal enterprise masquerading as a legitimate state. Tougher still to point this out to the Washington establishment, always enamored of tales of second chances and political redemption. It puts you in the position of being a sore loser. Worse, a sore loser with a failed political agenda. So it was as Ellen and I try to raise the alarm after Charles Taylor takes the presidency of Liberia.

Taylor is a master of theatrics, a chameleon, a charismatic charmer. He can proclaim his devotion to God and Christianity at a prayer breakfast attended by the likes of televangelist Pat Robertson and Reverend Jesse Jackson, and then that same week order the mutilation of young boys, their hands chopped off for some perceived defiance of his will. In a remote world with scarce modern communications and few journalists willing to expose themselves to the dangers of the sub-region, Taylor can let you see what he wants you to see, do the pantomime, continue the charade, convince you that he is just like his "brother from Ghana," Flight Lieutenant Jerry Rawlings.

Rawlings came to power through a military coup in 1979, but then resigned from the Air Force, formed a political party, ran for office, won the Ghanaian presidency fairly in a democratic election, and governed successfully with a national agenda for development. Rawlings ceremoniously exchanged a fountain pen for the pistol that he had always kept strapped to his ankle. He became the symbol of an African leader capable of a true democratic transition, from war to governance.

But as Ellen says repeatedly, "Charles Taylor is no Jerry Rawlings."

♦

I am not supposed to be working anymore on Liberia. Management at my newly reconstituted firm, Black, Kelly, Scruggs & Healey (BKSH), believes that I have "wasted the time and the resources of the company on a mission of mercy." Mercy is not a profitable endeavor, management notes. The single retainer billed to Ellen's support organization, the West Africa Child Development Fund, formed "to build support in the United States for a truly free and fair election in Liberia," has gone unpaid for more than eight months.

Every Monday morning, at 8:30 a.m., the BKSH professionals convene in the conference room, about twenty-two of us seated at the oval conference table of rich mahogany wood. The purpose of the weekly meetings is to go through the priorities for the week—with new business being the only priority. Charlie Black, the chairman, sits at the head of the table; the president, Scott Patrick, sits at the other end.

After Ellen lost the election, it has become a ritual in these meetings for Charlie and Scott to ask pointedly, "Is there any update on the collection of the Liberian monies?" And for months my reply is the same. I look right at Scott or Charlie, and supply a list of the people I have called and report in which country I believe the monies now reside and from which account they will soon be moved. I always close with an "even so" editorial emphasizing that the relationships we have built in Congress and the media during Ellen's campaign are an invaluable asset to the company and its other international clients.

By early 1998 I just keep my eyes downcast and answer, "No. No movement."

After Ellen's defeat, I return with urgency to the search for new business, trying to keep my "numbers" up. In the lobbying and public relations world, it all comes down to billable hours unless you are management or one of the recent political hires brought in to maintain political currency with contacts in the ever-shifting fortunes of Washington, DC. I am not part of that protected class. I have to maintain the 40 percent profit margin set by the parent company, Burson-Martseller.

Ellen has similar pressures. She needs to recreate a livelihood for herself after giving up her UN job—and the full value of her pension. So after the July elections, adamantly refusing to legitimize Taylor with her presence in his government, Ellen chooses to return to the neighboring West African nation of Côte d'Ivoire. There, she resurrects her nonpolitical career in banking and development as a partner with Stephen Cashin, whom she met at Equator Bank more than two decades earlier and who is now as much a family member as a business partner. Cashin will become one of the first major American investors to put capital at risk in post-conflict Liberia, opening the International Bank of Liberia (IB).

◆

Near the end of February 1998, six months after Taylor took office, I am sitting at my desk on the 8th floor of 1801 K Street when I receive a phone call from Ellen in Abidjan, the Ivorian capital. I put her on hold, shut my door, and return to the line. As she is no longer a client, with her bill still unpaid, it is best to keep the call private.

I am greeted by the familiar static that accompanies all her calls from West Africa. This time though, I find no irritation in the crackling line. It feels more like a welcoming back. I am so happy to hear her voice!

Ellen has seen a *Washington Times* op-ed by Donald Payne, Democratic member of Congress from New Jersey. Congressman Payne is calling for President Bill Clinton to offer Charles Taylor an official visit to the White House with full honors—a State Visit.

"Have you read the *Washington Times* article, Riva?" asks Ellen, the agitation in her voice overcoming the static on the line. "It's one thing to validate this charade of an election, but quite another to give the man White House honors and legitimize his policies of plunder and regional destabilization!"

I spin my chair around, look out the window at the K Street traffic, and start taking notes. I take notes all the time. I am never without a notebook. It is like an appendage, full of scribbles that are illegible, unintelligible and useless to anyone but me.

"I have written a rejoinder to the article, which I am sending to you now, and I want to have it published," she instructs. "Ninety percent of state resources are going through illegal, criminal channels to support Taylor's cronies and build up his personal army." She pauses, for a moment, and then continues, "Riva, there are 250,000 displaced persons who have not been repatriated or given basic food and shelter while Taylor sends hundreds of his troops to Burkina Faso and Libya for training. He is purchasing millions of dollars of weapons. My rejoinder is detailed and I am challenging the position of Mr. Payne."

I understand and share Ellen's outrage, but there is a major obstacle to her plan. An argumentative rebuttal to an article written by a US congressman and a respected leader of the Congressional Black Caucus is just a really bad idea.

"Ellen, it's the wrong way to go," I respond.

"But the facts are irrefutable, Riva," she insists.

"I realize that, Ellen. But you're just going to come across as an angry opponent of Taylor who lost to him in the last election. Taylor will discredit your message as an empty political attack," I reply. "And publicly challenging a distinguished member of the Congressional Black Caucus is not going to score us any points."

There is prolonged silence on the line, which indicates that Ellen is listening.

"Can you come to Washington?" I ask. "We need documentation of what you are alleging in your article. Face-to-face meetings will have more impact. Plus, the deteriorating situation in Sierra Leone is beginning to get Washington's attention, specifically, the increasing number of credible, eye-witness reports that Taylor is supplying the Revolutionary United Front (RUF) in Sierra Leone—with gruesome effect. We need to get Congress more facts, more eye-witness accounts, irrefutable evidence."

Sierra Leone has become a hell worse than that of Liberia, even at the height of its civil wars. The killing of civilians by the Revolutionary

United Front (RUF), in their attempt to unseat the popularly elected sitting president, Ahmed Kabbah, is not indiscriminate; it is systematic. The RUF itself terms its cleansing operation "No Living Thing." Human rights organizations report that the campaign of rape, amputation and mutilation is the worst ever seen on the continent, next to the outright genocide in Rwanda. It is posited at the time that the RUF models itself after Taylor, trying to re-create his campaign of fear to cow a defenseless civilian population into submission.

Taylor and RUF leader Foday Sankoh have been allies since 1992. But now Taylor can intervene as a sovereign, the elected president of Liberia. One can only imagine what that will mean to the Sierra Leonean people.

"I'll come prepared," declares Ellen. "Let's work on a date in early April after the Easter holidays." The call ends and I re-open my office door. I'm happy—I get to see Ellen again. But between now and then I have to pay attention to my numbers. And in a twist of client fate, that will mean a return to Equatorial Guinea.

◆

My relationship, and that of BKSH, with President Obiang has its challenges, because we tell our clients what they do not want to hear. This sometimes leads to productive developments, and sometimes to the termination of our contract.

In the case of Equatorial Guinea, we argue in formal, diplomatic parlance that "material changes on the ground in Equatorial Guinea on the issues of democracy and human rights are what will improve the country's bilateral relationship with the United States." We continue to search out partnerships for the government with reputable NGOs, just as we did during the election with the Washington-based *International Foundation for Electoral Systems (IFES),* despite their unwelcome criticism of the process. We also continue to lay out plans for private US contractors to help professionalize President Obiang's military. We argue that "while we wait for the US to consider Foreign Military Assistance, the government should seek out private support in the meantime. It shows good intention and commitment to a force that respects the civilian population."

While these recommendations are not unwelcome, and indeed some of them, like the hiring of professional security contractors, are even adopted eventually, what President Obiang really wants is an Oval Office meeting. That, we know, will not happen—at least not for a while. We push back. We explain that in our system of government in the US, the most important officer in the bilateral relationship is actually the State Department Desk Officer, the person who moves the cable traffic, controls the information flow and therefore defines the agenda. You can bypass that person, we explain, but any policy decision review will always end up on his or her desk.

"You build from the bottom of the pyramid," I explain to this president who exercises near-absolute power. Although an accurate and realistic statement, it is also the wrong answer. We soon find ourselves replaced by another firm who promises to go "right to the top."

But the beauty of the advocacy business is that expertise and contacts can always be recycled and put to good use. So it is in Equatorial Guinea when the bourgeoning US business community, with 1,500 employees and contractors in-country, makes it a priority to re-open the US Embassy in the capital city of Malabo. The embassy has been closed two years because of federal budget cuts compounded by a deteriorating relationship with the Obiang government.

Dallas-based Triton Energy, a small company that looks at Africa's frontier basins and tries to find oil that the super majors overlooked or didn't have the creativity to imagine, hires us to work on their behalf. Triton is expected to drill its first exploratory well in 1999 in the Ceiba Field, off the coast of Equatorial Guinea, just two years after obtaining the acreage. They do not have time for the Washington bureaucracy to operate at its usual, plodding pace in re-considering its decision to close the US embassy. "If you lose your passport, or if it is stolen, it will take you upwards of three weeks to figure out how to get home," recounts one petroleum engineer who knows from experience.

Not a lot of people in Washington can say that they have ever been to Malabo, or even know where it is. So there is little competition for the project work. Partnering with the business community in Equatorial Guinea is great for me because it frees me from a direct relationship with President Obiang and his government, and the psychological weight that such a relationship carries, particularly after my principled work with Ellen. At the same time, it enables me to maintain my numbers and profit margin. Further, it allows me to argue the principle of US economic and business interests, pointing out the absurdity of closing a US Embassy in a country where American investors have just pumped in $5 billion and there are still no consular services for American citizens in the country. It is a clinically logical case to make, not emotional, not one associated with life or death; I welcome the assignment.

In the coalition are Mobil Oil Corporation, Ocean Energy, CMS Nomeco, Samedan Oil, Axem Resources, Globex, MOE Oil & Gas, Oceaneering, the Howell Group, Dolan International, Frederick R. Harris, Triton Energy, McDermott Engineering, Foster Wheeler and Raytheon Engineers and Constructors—all in all, an impressive, powerful group.

But it is Jim Musselman, Triton's CEO, who leads the effort and steals the show wherever he goes. Jim is six foot two, with a broad sturdy physique, freckles dotting his balding head, a broad smile, and a voice oozing with Texas charm. He wears cowboy boots wherever he goes, which gives him an additional two inches. Under Jim's leadership, the lobbying effort is eventually successful, as is Triton's exploration in the Ceiba Field. Triton's leadership would later reconstitute under the name of Kosmos Energy and discover the Jubilee Field in Ghana. But it is my faltering relationship with President Obiang that gets me on the ground floor working with Triton and the other American companies. It is what I have always loved, and dreaded, about the lobbying and public relations business: You never know what is coming around the corner.

◆

It is just after Easter when Ellen returns to Washington, her first working trip since Charles Taylor was elected. Because the Clinton Administration is winding down its second term, and more relevant, because they have stood behind the vote that put Charles Taylor into office and are vested in the status quo, I feel there is very little value in doing an "I told you so" to Susan Rice, the assistant secretary of state for African affairs, and Special Envoy Jeter. Instead, I give priority to the meetings program in the Congress. Congressman Donald Payne will be our first stop.

It is important for Ellen to appeal directly to Congressman Payne who appears to be advocating for Taylor's administration after his February 27 *Washington Times* article. Despite our frustrations with him, his voice matters greatly in the debate on African policy. He has a passionate commitment to the continent even though he mistakes Taylor for a pan-Africanist, the image that Taylor presents to the world, and fails to see him for the felon that he is. The other pivot point in Congress will be Ed Royce, who has no such illusions about Taylor. As chairman of the Africa Subcommittee, he has the ability to hold hearings and demand attention and accountability in Liberia.

Ellen and I are ushered into Congressman Payne's office. His desk is centered between two floor-to-ceiling windows and we have to squint through the glare to get a clear look at the Congressman. Ellen goes through the points of her unpublished op-ed on Taylor's destruction of the Liberian state. She speaks almost in monotone, as if fearful, I think, to show her disappointment with the Congressman's position.

Says Ellen, "Backroom deals and unregulated monopolies gifted to business partners, including those in the regional states that assured his coming to power, have crowded out bona fide entrepreneurs. The working economy has collapsed."

She explains that nothing has been done to help those displaced from the war and that there have been no improvements in nutrition, sanitation, education, housing or welfare. "Until such time as Taylor demonstrates that he is committed to democracy, the rule of law, the development of Liberia and to the welfare of the Liberian people," Ellen declares, "US monies should be withheld unless they are going to humanitarian organizations."

Payne jots down notes continuously. We are having an impact, I think.

Ellen also goes through the detailed intelligence she has received about Taylor's support of the RUF in Sierra Leone, the fact that Taylor is interested only in "settling scores with his enemies, increasing the spoils of plunder, now in Sierra Leone, and defining who his neighbors should be."

Congressman Payne listens intently to Ellen. Neither he nor his staff has the facts or ability to refute what she says. So the Congressman does the only thing he can to respond.

"I am going to get Charles Taylor on the phone," he announces, "and let you take up these matters directly with him."

As Congressman Payne starts to dial, Ellen all but leaps out of her chair and gestures to hang up the phone. I think that she might grab the receiver, but she does not.

"I know what he will say, Congressman," declares Ellen. "He will deny my concerns and say that I cannot accept the election loss. But this is not true. What I cannot accept is the suffering of the Liberian people."

Payne obviously did not anticipate Ellen's strong reaction to a direct call to Taylor in her presence. I am stunned that he seems to have Taylor on speed dial. After a brief pause, Payne says, "Ellen, please leave these issues with me. I will reach out to President Taylor with your concerns and get back to you."

The Congressman rises from his desk. The meeting is over.

Chairman Royce can't see us that afternoon and Ellen is not pleased. But I am able to secure a meeting for Ellen with Royce's senior staff, Tom Sheehy and Greg Simpkins.

"It is the staff that makes everything happen in Congress," I explain to Ellen. "They organize the meetings, conduct the research, plan the hearings, write floor speeches, draft the legislation, and ultimately define a forward strategy to impact US policy." Ellen looks skeptical but she will later come to appreciate this point.

Ellen dedicates her meeting with Greg and Tom to detailing Charles Taylor's actions since assuming office and his stepped up support for the RUF in Sierra Leone. Ellen explains that Charles Taylor's forces, the National Patriotic Front of Liberia (NPLF) are providing direct tactical support to the RUF. "The NPLF is being paid in US dollars to conduct certain risky military operations that the RUF will not consider," Ellen explains. "The forces co-mingle. Taylor has established safe havens across the border and is giving sanctuary to the RUF in Liberia."

Tom and Greg announce that they will suggest to the chairman that he hold a hearing in early summer to draw out the information and get the Clinton Administration on the record. This is a solid accomplishment for our meetings program, particularly after the disappointment with Congressman Payne.

♦

After Ellen returns to Côte d'Ivoire, it is up to me to coordinate the hearing and seek as much documented evidence as I can from our sources. And that proves very difficult. Although we know what Taylor is doing, the remoteness of the terrain, the complete insecurity of the area and its inaccessibility to Western journalists and human rights activists make any allegations very difficult to verify. Those who are there and bear witness are too afraid for themselves and their families to give evidence.

On June 11, 1998, Congressman Ed Royce opens the hearing of the Subcommittee on Africa of the House International Relations Committee of the 105th Congress. He titles it, "Reconstructing Sierra Leone," but the unspoken agenda is to bring to light the crimes of the RUF and the complicity of the Liberian president, Charles Taylor.

The Administration witness is Deputy Assistant Secretary of State for African Affairs Johnnie Carson. Carson would come to realize that State's intelligence on Taylor in 1998 was stale, and he would later correct that error. Carson will go on to become President Obama's Assistant Secretary of State for African Affairs and ultimately prove to be a great friend to Liberia. But today he is giving the administration's line on Taylor, and that sets the tone of the hearing. No one debates the brutality of the RUF, Carson states, but "the RUF has no political support or identifiable constituencies. This gang-like outfit is motivated only by greed and the sheer quest for power."

Chairman Royce asks Carson, "Is the Liberian government actively intervening in Sierra Leone?" His follow-up question is "And if so, what is the US government prepared to do to stop this interference?"

"We have no proof or evidence that the Liberian government has been intervening in Sierra Leone," states Carson. "We, like you, have heard reports, but nothing has been confirmed. We have received assurances from the government of Liberia that they are not in any way providing arms or material for the combatants. We continue to monitor the situation closely. I might add," continues Carson, "that to show his good faith in this, the Liberian president indicated at one point last month that he was prepared to allow Nigeria and ECOMOG troops to work with the government and monitor the border."

Congressman Robert Menendez, (D-NJ), the Ranking Democrat on the Subcommittee finds Carson's comments implausible and presses him further. "So, again, you see none of the surrounding States providing assistance or solace to the RUF?" asks Menendez.

"We are monitoring it closely," replies Carson.

Menendez comes at it again, "And you know of no support at all to the RUF?"

"To date, we know of none," closes out Carson.

Carson has taken all the oxygen out of the room, and a very skeptical Royce closes the first panel of witnesses.

◆

My report back to Ellen is not a pleasant one. I shut my office door and give her the blow-by-blow. She is particularly upset about Ambassador Carson's last comment implying that somehow Taylor is part of the solution. Despite her disappointment with the outcome of the hearing, I am relieved that Ellen is not disappointed in me.

"You made the hearing happen, Riva. It is our own failure that we do not have the documentation that shows Taylor's complicity with the RUF's crimes in Sierra Leone. Until we get it, he will not be stopped."

I take a deep breath, spin my chair once, then again.

"We'll get it done," I say to Ellen, battling back the sense of hopelessness that is creeping in. "We can move the US government, I think, but it is going to take overwhelming proof."

The line goes dead. "We'll get it done," I repeat into the void.

SIX

IS WASHINGTON LISTENING?

Washington, DC, to Ouagadougou, Burkina Faso
1999–2002

From her exile in Côte d'Ivoire, Ellen takes up her new position as a board member of the Modern Africa Growth Fund, a Washington-based investment fund with debt from the US government's Overseas Private Investment Corporation (OPIC). It is the very early days of portfolio investment on the continent. The potential for double-digit return is there. But you have to have a tolerance for risk—commercial and the unforeseen political.

One of Modern Africa's investments is in Cora de Comstar, the first cell phone company in Côte d'Ivoire to establish connectivity across the country, even in the north where anti-government rebels continue to find sanctuary against the sitting president, Laurent Gbagbo, who came to power one year earlier. Unfortunately for Modern Africa's investors, Cora de Comstar is a strategic asset that proves to be just too attractive for the insecure Ivoirian president, who lives in constant fear of a counterinsurgency. In early 2000, through a corrupt court order enforced by his presidential police, Gbagbo seizes the US-owned company.

But there is a silver lining to this expropriation, at least for me. Ellen has not been able to pay off the fee she owes BKSH for its efforts—my efforts, actually—on her behalf as a candidate. So I have to figure out a way to continue my pro-bono work for her, if not with the full support of my company and its partners, at least with their tacit acceptance. Now, in response to the move by Gbagbo, Ellen finds a new client for me, and thus for BKSH. To a consortium of American investors, including Modern Africa and Western Wireless International (WWI), Ellen announces, "What you need is a good lobbyist in Washington, DC." She goes on to explain to Brad Horwitz, WWI's president, "You need someone to make sure that the government of Côte d'Ivoire knows that there is a price to be paid for their treatment of US investors. You need to pick a very public and costly fight with the government."

Brad is one of the pioneers in the wireless business, along with his Seattle-based partner, John Stanton. Their model, not unlike that of Triton, is to "go where no one else would even consider." Brad lives his life on the edge, exactly where he seems most comfortable. His portfolio reflects a high tolerance for risk—Ghana, Haiti, Bolivia, the Republic of Georgia, Slovenia and Côte d'Ivoire.

Getting straight to the point of Ellen's diplo-speak, Brad summarizes, "So essentially we need to become such a pain in the ass that Gbagbo will do anything to make us go away. If Riva can do that," he concludes, "she's hired."

The case of Cora de Comstar becomes a legend in the annals of US State Department commercial diplomacy. We pick a very public and painful fight with the Ivoirians. Côte d'Ivoire becomes the first African country since the enactment of the Africa Growth and Opportunity Act (AGOA), passed in 2000, to lose the trade preference made available under the act. Shortly thereafter, Gbagbo's government does end up paying WWI to go away, compensating the company for the loss of its investment. Gbagbo's political career comes to an abrupt end a few years later when he is charged with four counts of crimes against humanity. He is extradited to the International Criminal Court, The Hague, in 2011 to stand trial for his complicity in the death of thousands of civilians killed during peaceful democratic protests.

I tell Ellen that my work against Gbagbo and the resulting US decision to terminate trade preference for Côte d'Ivoire has created a whole new list of enemies for me.

"You should consider all of the enemies you accumulate as a badge of honor," Ellen replies. "That is how I view mine."

◆

A lot has happened in Liberia in the one year since the Congressional hearing of June 1998, and all of it bad. "It was all predictable," as far as Ellen is concerned, "and all of it preventable."

At the time, I thought our effort a failure. But the investigation establishes a baseline of concern, and Congressman Royce and his staff are unrelenting. On May 11, 1999, Royce convenes another hearing on the instability in Sierra Leone, this time to consider House Resolution 62, "to address the tragic situation in Sierra Leone where the elected President, Ahmed Kabbah, is under siege by rebel forces." HR 62 calls for an end to hostilities and condemns "the gross human rights violations committed." The resolution names 'names,' identifying President Charles Taylor as providing "direct military assistance to the rebel forces."

In contrast to one year earlier and the "we have no proof" comment, at Royce's second hearing, the State Department is in full agreement with the facts on the ground as we know them, and report the same to the House International Relations Committee: "The government of Liberia continues to actively support the rebels in Sierra Leone, including the provision of arms and ammunition."

But even with official US confirmation of Taylor's role in regional destabilization, many of the House Democrats, including Payne, Barbara Lee (D-CA), Gregory Meeks (D-NY) and the Republican Member from the 12th District of California, Tom Campbell, press for an amendment to HR 62 *not* to identify specific guilty parties, including Mr. Taylor. There remains an attachment to Taylor, reluctance by these members to recognize him for who he is, or at a minimum, what he has become, and what he is capable of.

Responding to the proposed amendment, Royce says, "I do not think for the sake of diplomatic niceties we should avoid trying to bring pressure to bear in order to resolve this crisis. This is a crisis in which people are having their arms amputated, defenseless civilians of all ages are being slaughtered, women are being raped, the wanton killing of innocents … I think it is absolutely essential that we go forward and do just that—apply pressure at the pressure points. I think we need to resist this amendment."

The amendment fails and the resolution passes. It names Charles Taylor, charging complicity in crimes against the people of Sierra Leone. That House Subcommittee hearing on Africa turns out to be a pivot point. From May 11, 1999, onward, the effort to hold Taylor accountable is never again partisan, but fully bipartisan and bicameral. Payne would later become an advocate for ending Liberia's civil war, and as president, Ellen would name a primary school after the congressman in Montserrado County.

In August of 2000, the United Nations Security Council passes Resolution 1315 requesting that the UN Secretary General negotiate with the government of Sierra Leone to set up a special court to prosecute individuals responsible for serious violations of international humanitarian law and national law committed in the territory of Sierra Leone since November 30, 1996. The court is finally codified internationally and in Sierra Leone law nearly two years later.

Ellen understands that the court can become the tool to de-legitimize Charles Taylor, to take away what the 1997 internationally recognized election has given to him: legitimacy as a sovereign. "War alone cannot unseat Taylor," Ellen tells me. "He must be stripped of his authority in the eyes of the Liberian people and the world." Like many others involved in humanitarian advocacy on the continent, Ellen learns from the Rwanda experience and the failure of the world to respond to the mass killings, the importance of talking in terms that mobilize the West—genocide and crimes against humanity. The Special Court of Sierra Leone can assemble the individual criminal acts into a larger narrative. It can label them war crimes and crimes against humanity.

There are many ironies of the sub-regional conflict. One of the greatest is that it will not be Taylor's offenses in Liberia that seal his fate, nor the loss of territorial control in the north and south of the country, nor the bands of anti-government forces that will later advance toward the capital city of Monrovia. It will be Taylor's interference in Sierra Leone that sows the seeds of his demise. Ultimately, he will be held accountable for crimes against the people of Sierra Leone, not those committed against his own people.

Now it becomes a matter of equipping the court with resources—the ability to collect forensic evidence, to interview and protect witnesses. There is another essential element and we cannot succeed without it: funding. According to its charter, the Special Court of Sierra Leone is to be funded 100 percent by voluntary contributions. So Ellen sends me back to Congress—back to Ed Royce's staff (who have continued to monitor the deteriorating situation in the sub-region almost as closely as Ellen and I do), back to the authorizers of foreign affairs and foreign relations and the appropriators of foreign operations assistance in the House and the Senate.

Over the past few years, Ellen has gained a true appreciation of the power that congressional staff wields and their importance in Washington policymaking. She never again expresses disappointment if we meet with Tim Rieser instead of Senator Leahy, or Tom Sheehy, Greg Simpkins and Malik Chaka instead of Congressman Royce, with Pearl Alice Marsh in lieu of Congressman Tom Lantos, with Lester Munson and Tom Callahan and not their boss, Congressman Benjamin Gilman, or with Jodi Christianson, not Congressman Robert Menendez. When Ellen later becomes president of Liberia, these congressional staffers are among the first people she thanks.

Things are progressing—more slowly than we wish, but progress is progress. A coalition of NGOs and peace activists, Liberia Watch, is formed by Vivian Lowery Derryck, former head of Africa for the US Agency for International Development (USAID). They add a powerful voice. International journalists also become relentless in their efforts to expose Charles Taylor's crimes. Douglas Farah, West Africa Bureau Chief of the *Washington Post* writes on June 5, 2002, "As long as Taylor is in power in Liberia, West Africa runs the risk of being a failed region. He is a threat not just at home, but for spreading conflict far beyond his borders, as he has already amply shown."

On September 23, 2002, Congress passes the Foreign Relations Act of 2003, which appropriates $5 million for the Special Court of Sierra Leone. While the monies are not sufficient, the Congressional appropriation has a catalytic impact on donor pledges to the court. And Congress will continue to fund the Special Court when other international pledges run dry.

◆

Beyond holding Taylor accountable, Ellen understands that the Liberian opposition to Taylor needs to gain the confidence of international stakeholders, to demonstrate that they are capable of uniting the country and administering it competently. Without a roadmap to return Liberia to a point of economic and political stability, the international community, itself so destabilized after the attacks of September 11, 2001, will not waste time on a regional African conflict. And there is the added irony that the last international plan formulated for Liberia, the deployment of a Nigerian force loyal to Taylor followed by the hasty 1997 elections, delivered the current tragedy to Liberia and the sub-region.

If there is going to be a new plan, Ellen will have to devise it. From her vantage point in Abidjan, with support from Conmany Wesseh, a prominent human rights activist from Liberia, she sets out to design a post-Taylor political landscape. Conmany was forced to flee the country in October 2000 after an attempt on his life. With the help of Amnesty International, he made it to the US for medical treatment, then moved to Abidjan to work with Ellen. Still recovering from a deep gash on his head, and intermittent headaches and nausea as a result, Conmany works full-time from a windowless cubbyhole in the Modern Africa office. He and Ellen, along with Edward McClain, Ellen's close friend and political ally, begin to put together a platform for the unification of the Liberian political parties and the restoration of civil society.

The trio calls on every contact they have collected over the past decade—business leaders, human rights activists, NGOs, political leaders—to find a regional host for a meeting of a unified Liberian opposition. The goal is to craft a document that will provide a consensus path for a return to peace in Liberia. In a diplomatic breakthrough they convince Blaise Compaoré, the president of Burkina Faso and an early backer of Taylor, to host on Burkina soil a meeting of Liberian leaders. No doubt, this will be viewed as a provocation by Taylor. But Compaoré calculates that Taylor's capacity to destabilize his country is minimal. Meanwhile, hosting the meeting will buy Compaoré much needed goodwill in the West. As Conmany Wesseh adeptly summarizes it, "Blaise needs to make up to the Liberian people for his early support of Taylor." Compaoré will manage to remain in power until 2014—27 years as president—when, ignoring strong domestic and international pressure, he tries to amend the constitution to prolong his hold on power yet further. Violence erupts and he subsequently flees the country.

Among the people Ellen turns to is George Soros, whom Ellen knew from serving on the board of the Open Society Initiative for West Africa (OSIWA). Soros makes a generous and critical donation to the DC-based International Republican Institute (IRI), the NGO of the Republican Party, so IRI can serve as the convener of the meeting in the Burkina Faso capital of Ouagadougou. The presence of IRI provides an unofficial US platform for the meeting, and a much-needed vehicle for funding staff, logistics, and transportation.

On July 11, 2002, the Liberian Leadership Forum convenes in Ouagadougou. Although sometimes considered a footnote in ending Liberia's conflict, it is in fact a diplomatic triumph, bringing together 14 political parties, a dozen Liberian and regional civil society organizations, the armed opposition, local media, and observers from the Economic Community of West African States (ECOWAS), along with diplomatic missions based in Ouagadougou.

At the close of the three-day meeting, the Ouagadougou declaration is signed. It calls for an immediate ceasefire between the government forces of President Charles Taylor and the rebel group LURD; the deployment of an international security stabilization force to take charge of security throughout the country and to monitor the ceasefire; the disarmament and demobilization of government and rebel troops; restructuring and retraining Liberia's military and its paramilitary forces; establishing a mechanism to manage peace-building and the democratic process; and holding free and fair elections according to international standards. It further requests "the creation of an international Contact Group to comprise Nigeria, Senegal, Burkina Faso, the United States, France and the United Kingdom" and makes an appeal "for the cooperation and support of the Liberian government, the Mano River Union, ECOWAS, the African Union and the European Union. It is envisaged that the Contact Group will take the lead in mobilizing the support of the international community for the peace plan." The accord will become the basis of a comprehensive peace one year later in Accra, Ghana.

My mission is to get the world to pay attention. The Liberian leaders have a plan and it will work. The opposition is unified and prepared to govern. International intervention through disarmament and peacekeeping is essential.

I blast-email the final declaration across Washington to our friends in Congress and to a reluctant Bush State Department that seems hardly in need of another task on its plate. I follow up with phone calls and meetings, and share articles that demonstrate "growing endorsements" from other Western democracies, including a statement from French Foreign Minister Dominique de Villepin: "We support the idea of a Contact Group which will be able to encourage a true resolution to this crisis."

Six days after the meeting, Ellen calls me to confirm that the declaration has been sent out and to get any reactions and feedback.

"What have you managed to accomplish Riva?" Ellen asks, without a hello, how are you?

"I sent the Ouagadougou declaration to the journalists who you met on your last visit," I reply, "including George Gedda of the Associated Press, Gus Constantine at the *Washington Times*, VOA's James Butty, and Andy Mosher of the *Washington Post,* and to Assistant Secretary of State for African Affairs Walter Kansteiner."

But I have to admit to Ellen, "I don't think Walter is likely to be proactive on this. He's a business guy. And even if Walter brings it to the attention of his senior deputies at State, and Liberia actually makes it onto the inter-agency agenda, there is just so much going on as we near the first anniversary of September 11. I don't see the administration prioritizing an international intervention force in Liberia. It doesn't mean we relax the pressure, but we need to be realistic."

My caution about the Bush administration and its reluctance to take on another foreign policy challenge does not seem to sink in with Ellen. She hears what I say, but she does not accept it.

"If we don't think six months ahead, we will just go backwards," Ellen insists. "Ultimately we will need the US military and the leadership of the Pentagon to back up any African stabilization force. That's your next mission."

Ellen is nothing if not driven. When it comes to serving her country, she is never afraid to think big. But the US military? The Pentagon?

"I am not optimistic that we can pull this off," I tell her. "There are real national security challenges with the on-going coalition war in Afghanistan against the Taliban." There is also another, more ominous factor, which I do not convey then to Ellen. It's Washington's worst-kept secret. There will soon be another American war, this time against Saddam Hussein in Iraq.

"I believe we are going to have to rely, like we always have, on Congress to keep Liberia on the agenda, at least for now," I tell Ellen.

Six months later, February 14, Valentine's Day, there is still no progress on US backing for an African stabilization force. Ellen is deeply frustrated. She writes:

"The news today is that war is once again starting at the Liberian border with Sierra Leone. We are not surprised because we were aware that arms and men were being moved by Taylor to the Sierra Leone border city of Robertsport a few months ago. All should realize that with his apparent success in Côte d'Ivoire, Taylor is more emboldened and is well advanced in preparation to move again into Sierra Leone. The man is true to his word a couple of years ago [when he said] that if rejected by the international community he would ensure that the entire West African sub-region felt his power through a destabilization [and it] would take ten years to restore things to normal."

She closes her note with an emphatic question that has become her refrain to me.

"Is Washington listening???"

Riva with MSNBC camera crew at Saddam Hussein's parade ground, Baghdad, May 2003.

SEVEN

THE IRAQ CONNECTION

Bagdad, Iraq
May, 2003

There are a number of things to love and to hate about the lobbying and public relations business. Sometimes you find yourself obliged to polish the image of some pretty unsavory characters, hoping all the while that your efforts will lead ultimately to some greater good, or at least that a worse evil will be avoided. You plunge ahead, doing the job you signed on to do. Then, more rarely, someone like Ellen comes along. Working for her is a privilege, not a task—rewarding, even exhilarating.

But whatever else you can say about this business, it has plenty of surprises in store. You might be tasked with some dull, low-consequence commercial fix, requiring a narrow ruling by a single congressional committee. Or you might be thrust into the middle of a major US foreign policy decision that divides the American public, divides America from its traditional allies, and leads to the deaths of many people, some of them innocent, some of them not.

The invasion of Iraq and the overthrow of Saddam Hussein is an example.

While Ellen impatiently waits out her exile in Côte d'Ivoire, monitoring the increasingly bold military adventures of Charles Taylor in Liberia and his successful efforts to destabilize neighboring states, the US government turns its main focus to the foreign policy strategies that will come to define the administration of George W. Bush. During the run-up to the war in Iraq, and in the first heady weeks and months of the invasion, Liberia and Charles Taylor fall far down the list of priorities for the Bush White House. There is a much bigger prize at stake.

As typically happens, these major foreign policy events are years in the making. On October 31, 1998, that President Clinton signed the Iraq Liberation Act of 1998, H.R. 4655, sent to him by the Republican-controlled Congress. It declared that it should henceforth be the policy of the United States to seek to remove the Saddam Hussein regime from power in Iraq and to replace it with a democratic government. It authorized the President, after notifying specified congressional committees, to provide Iraqi democratic opposition organizations with: (1) grant assistance for radio and television broadcasting to Iraq; (2) Department of Defense (DOD) articles and services as well as military education and training (IMET); and (3) humanitarian assistance, with emphasis on addressing the needs of individuals who have fled from areas under the control of the Hussein regime. It also prohibited assistance to any group or organization engaged in military cooperation with the Hussein regime.

Seven months later, on May 21, 1999, President Clinton signed into law the Omnibus Consolidated and Emergency Supplemental Appropriations Act of 1999, which made $8 million available for assistance to the Iraqi democratic opposition, under the umbrella of the Iraqi National Congress (INC). This assistance was intended "to help the democratic opposition unify, work together more effectively, and articulate the aspirations of the Iraqi people for a pluralistic, participatory political system that will include all of Iraq's diverse ethnic and religious groups."

It was a noble sentiment, conveyed in language that few people could possibly object to, which is how most such legislation is written. But whatever it was, I had no idea at the time how profoundly this legislation would affect me, personally and professionally.

The INC was established under the leadership of Ahmed Chalabi in October of 1992 following the close of the first Gulf War. Its purpose was to bring together the opponents of Saddam Hussein in one platform dedicated to a pluralistic democracy in Iraq. It represented the first major attempt to unify the disparate forces at work in the country—Kurds, Sunni and Shi'ite Arabs, Islamic fundamentalists and secular Iraqis, as well as democrats, monarchists, nationalists, ex-military officers and no doubt members of other groups too.

While President Clinton signed the law, his administration had no intention of being dragged into a proxy confrontation created by the Republican Congress through the INC. A major directive of the Iraq Liberation Act—the provision of spare Department of Defense surplus, actual weaponry—would remain dormant as it went through a long, slow bureaucratic review. But other aspects of the legislation were put out to competitive bid, such as technical support to the INC to help them develop a unified message platform and capacity. This was an effort to show Congress that there was political will to implement some aspects of the law. That is where I came in.

My company, BKSH, in partnership with our parent company, Burson-Marstellar, competed for the US State Department contract. We had the competencies, with an office in London where many of the players in the Iraq opposition were based. And not insignificantly, our firm had the strong support of the Republican Senate Foreign Relations Committee and its chairman, Senator Jesse Helms, in part because our own chairman, Charlie Black, was a senior Republican operative. We won the contract. I became the project manager.

I commuted to London where our team in the UK and I tried to create unified messages and policies for the opposition, despite the fact that most of the players hated one another. But there were big changes ahead, for the INC and the world. George W. Bush was elected president. Then 9/11 happened.

The assignment started out as a relatively benign and remote exercise in public relations, dateline London, with the usual press releases drawing attention to the latest human rights reports by the State Department cataloguing Saddam's abuses of the non-Sunni elite. It turned into a project of historical consequence, of great personal and professional risk to me, and put me in the middle of one of the greatest foreign policy firestorms since Vietnam.

♦

Although much of my professional focus now turns to Iraq and the INC, Ellen is never out of my thoughts. On March 7, 2003, the Special Court of Sierra Leone indicts Charles Taylor on 17 counts of crimes against the people of the neighboring country of Sierra Leone. The docket is sealed until June, to allow the international community time to figure out what to do with Charles Taylor now that the Court has ruled.

But even with the court ruling and the Ouagadougou Accords, there is little hope of a major intervention that involves American troops in Liberia. In the larger scheme of things, and in the global priorities of the Bush administration, Liberia is a small country in Africa suffering the ravages of war. But 6,200 miles away there is a bigger country of immense strategic significance to the US, with a villain of greater consequence in power. Soon tens of thousands of American troops will be present on its soil.

Charles Taylor will have to wait. So will Ellen.

On March 19, 2003, President Bush launches Operation Iraqi Freedom. Less than two months later, on May 8, 2003, I will convoy into the war zone of Iraq. Not exactly legal. Probably not very smart. But at the time, I thought it was essential.

♦

What am I doing here?

It is a question that I really don't want to ask myself. If I second-guess my decision it could further undermine my already wobbly confidence. It is May 9, 2003, six o'clock in the morning, 92 degrees. I am in a convoy of three vehicles heading through Kuwait on our way to the war zone of Iraq. I am in the backseat of a Toyota SUV, wedged between two Rambo-like men—Len and Mike—both seasoned correspondents for NBC. They are relaxed, almost laidback with a "been there, done that" attitude about heading into a war zone. Events are moving quickly. Saddam Hussein is on the run. The US Marines have taken control of Baghdad.

Four days ago I was worried about forgetting to buy M&Ms for my son Andrew's sixth birthday cake. Yesterday, I was told firmly by a Kuwaiti physician not to travel because of a severe bacterial infection in my stomach. Today, I am trying to remember the warnings from the journalists I spoke with last night at the Kuwaiti Sheraton. "Do not stop or get out of the car when you cross the border. Opportunistic mobs will ambush you, strip you of all your belongings, and probably steal the car, too."

I am desperately trying not to focus on the cramping in my belly. My intrepid traveling companions intimated that my discomfort was probably "nerves," due to my being a woman and all. Mike even hinted that I was starving myself and had an eating disorder.

What am I doing here?

We were up at 3:00 am this morning, packed by 4:00, and left our hotel at 5:00. The highway through Kuwait is peppered with warehouses, businesses, and gas stations, but as we near the Iraqi border, all signs of life disappear. Almost two hours into our journey and the temperature is climbing toward 100 degrees. We were also told at the hotel to expect some delays at the border. We had all the necessary papers to enter smoothly: valid passports, Kuwaiti visas, and the all-important letter from the Ministry of Information allowing us to cross into Iraq.

We arrive at the border crossing and just beyond, on the Iraqi side, I can see a crowd of men lining the highway, poised and waiting. After handing over our papers to the Kuwaiti border patrol agent, we are informed that our Kuwaiti drivers don't have official letters. Therefore, we can go on, but not our drivers. That, we try to explain, would be a disaster. As we argue with the guard, the Head Kuwaiti Patrol Officer approaches our convoy with a cocky saunter. His body language conveys a clear message. He is in charge in this barren desert landscape and we had better tow the line. He'll keep us here as long as he wants. Sizing him up, I determine he is in his late 50s and obviously enjoys the power he wields in this little sandy corner of the world. He wears a constant smirk, speaks perfect English, and acts like a man who fancies himself attractive, potbelly and all.

I grab Tresha Marble, a producer with Discovery Channel, the only other woman in the convoy. We are about the same size and both of us understand the value of being a woman in certain sticky situations that require a particular kind of female diplomacy. If anyone can get us across the border, it will have to be us.

We join the Head Patrol Officer in his office and begin to coax, cajole, threaten, and even flirt—whatever it takes—to get us through. It is obvious that he is amused that two women have any interest at all in going into the chaos and danger of Iraq. We share water and biscuits with him. We sprinkle the conversation with the names of important members of the Kuwaiti ministry, and Tresha eventually places a phone call to a senior Kuwaiti official who speaks with him. All of this, he accepts without a trace of irritation. In fact, he appears to enjoy every second—the company of two pleading, manipulative women, and the ego-pumping thrill of holding up our convoy.

I will admit that it did occur to me, for a fleeting moment, that this could be my out. If we couldn't get into Iraq, at least I had tried. I could then head home to Jeff and my kids, recover from my illness, and call it a day. But I had to push this thought away. I couldn't let my ambivalence make an already difficult situation even more trying.

The Head Patrol Officer finally relents. We are allowed to cross into Iraq. Before we reach the rabid crowd, I search for our INC scout, Sabbah, who is scheduled to be waiting just beyond the border post. He has the local knowledge, training, and wherewithal to get us into Baghdad—hopefully in one piece. Standing next to a white transport vehicle, I spot a man well over six feet tall, at least 280 pounds, with moustache and dark olive skin, wearing a white caftan robe and brown sandals. He fits the description I was given by the INC—a description that included an AK-47 at the ready.

Approaching him, his eyes are fixed on me in a steely gaze. I slow to a halt and yell, "I'm Riva!" I had been told that he only speaks Arabic and German. I don't ask his name, waiting for him to announce himself. There are reports of Iraqis posing as facilitators who rob incoming travelers. He slaps his chest with his hand. "Sabbah," he says with deep, calm authority. The sound of his name is like a prayer of protection, an incantation of safety, and I feel immediately that Sabbah will surely deliver us to Baghdad with our limbs intact.

The Kuwaiti officials only patrol the area up to the gate. Our convoy lines up behind Sabbah's vehicle and we brace ourselves for the greeting we are about to receive from the hundreds of men and boys up ahead, a mere fifty feet from the border.

Welcome to Iraq.

Len barks at Mike to get as much footage of the upcoming pandemonium as possible as we take off behind Sabbah. I focus on our driver, Hassan, whom we are paying $3,000 to make the round-trip journey. Self-assured up until now, he suddenly tenses. His eyes widen as Sabbah guns it toward the crowd and races far ahead of our convoy.

I see Sabbah waving his arm out the window like a commanding sword, urging us to gas it and get through the mob quickly.

"Go! Hurry!" I shout.

Len and Mike seem unperturbed at first, but as the crush of bodies surrounds us, hands and fists pounding at the windows of our SUV, we all panic.

"Move it!" Len shouts at Hassan.

"Shit," Mike mutters. "Shit," he repeats, even as he continues to record. I turn and watch as the two cars behind us disappear from sight amid a throbbing pulse of marauding Iraqis.

From out of nowhere, Sabbah's white stallion appears. It plows through the crowd from the opposite direction, forcing the throng to scramble away from our vehicles. Sabbah motions to our driver to get us the hell out of there. Hassan hits the gas and we lurch forward as the Iraqis dive miraculously out of harm's way. I don't look back; my eyes are fixed on the blessed site of the clear, empty road ahead.

What am I doing here?

As soon as the question arises again, I shove it away, take a deep breath, and join Mike, Len, and Hassan in a round of jubilant high-fives. We made it.

So far.

We drive through the desert wasteland, grim and uninviting, mile after mile of endless sand and oppressive heat shimmering off the asphalt road. Completing the view, even punctuating the despair of the landscape, are rusted and rotted tanks and armored vehicles abandoned along the highway. These are the remnants of Saddam's failed military campaign against Kuwait. They look like monstrous war toys strewn and discarded by angry gods.

Another absurd sight, to my mind, that appears every twenty miles or so there is a rest stop consisting of cement umbrellas over cement benches. Does anyone ever stop to rest here? Does anyone ever sit under one of those umbrellas? In the middle of this desert, in this heat, those benches must reach 120 degrees Fahrenheit.

Two hours into Iraq, I begin to feel extremely sick. I sit in silence, repeating a mantra: *I won't make us stop*. I do not want to give Mike or Len any more ammunition for their theories about my condition. When I spoke with Jeff on the phone last night I didn't tell him about my trip to the Kuwaiti doctor, his diagnosis and warning that I should not travel. Not only would Jeff worry, he might try to pressure me into not going.

We are approaching *Nasiriyah,* the town where Private First Class Jessica Lynch was ambushed, brutally beaten, raped, and weeks later, dramatically rescued. I remember watching the drama unfold on national television and recall how, at the time, commentators wondered if scores more Americans would die in fierce resistance as our troops marched toward Baghdad. It had not occurred to me then that I might possibly be one of those Americans. My own doubts surface now. What if we were wrong? What if Saddam's resistance was fiercer than we anticipated? One journalist back in Kuwait had delivered dire news about *Nasiriyah.* The town was still dangerous, gangs of thieves set up barricades in the streets that forced cars to a halt. "Speed through there as fast as you can," he warned.

The streets narrow as we enter the town. Crowds of Iraqis are everywhere. Crumbling, bombed-out buildings, overturned cars, piles of garbage and debris are the visible signs of chaos and anarchy. We can see the rage on the faces of the townspeople. There is a sense of seething malice in the air. An anxious silence fills the car as Mike shoots footage and Hassan tries to keep up with Sabbah, who is so far ahead of us he is nearly out of sight.

We're not going to be robbed. We're going to be killed.

Suddenly a torrent of rocks and bricks smashes against the car. The explosive sounds blast up my spine. *This is it*, I think, *I'm going to die in*

Nasiriyah. Stoned to death! The place everyone wanted to escape from, and I've traveled here voluntarily! I won't be considered an American hero like the soldiers who came before me. Nor will people judge me like those journalists killed in the line of duty. There will be no sympathy. People will say I was just some PR hack that had no business being in a war zone anyway. And, of course, the State Department will put out a statement that I had no permission to be here. I was traveling without a proper waiver.

I bend forward and wrap my arms around my legs. As the rocks thunder against the car, I begin to count silently to myself. Images of Jeff, Kylie, and Andrew trip through my brain. *I'm so sorry*, I silently say to them, *I'm so sorry*.

The minutes feel like a century as our convoy finally races out of the town, only the echo of the stones and the taunting shouts in our wake. This time we don't share jubilant high-fives. We remain mostly quiet until we reach the outskirts of Baghdad.

When we finally stop, I get out of the car and vomit. By now, I don't give a shit what Len and Mike think.

Just outside of Baghdad we are stopped by a British Security Officer and instructed that we must wear our bulletproof vests and helmets for the rest of the trip. I haven't tried mine on. All our vests have been propped up against the vehicle doors as protection from bullets. These aren't the sleek, high-tech, lightweight body armor the US Army sported. Ours are antiques, perhaps circa WWII, and mine weighs about as much as I do. Len and Mike help me get it on and when they let go, my knees all but collapse underneath me. The helmet makes an equally poor showing. It is too small, and with my thick, curly hair, doesn't even cover my head.

Back in the car, I feel doomed. With our vests secured, I am squeezed between the guys, literally crushed by their vested bulk. I can't breathe, and my stomach continues its rumbling rebellion. I sip water to stave off dehydration, especially since I had unceremoniously emptied the contents of my stomach along the road. Adding to it all, the stiff vest presses directly against my bladder.

Think happy thoughts? Forget it. Chuck the vest out the window? Think bullets. Chuck out Len and Mike? Better.

Gripping my backpack with both hands, I mentally list its contents: passport, airline ticket, cash, medications, and my good luck charms. Kylie gave me a tattered piece of her favorite blanket, one that she has had since birth, and Andrew made me an early Mother's Day card, which reads: *I love you because you take good care of me. Love, Andrew.*

Fifteen kilometers later, approaching a military checkpoint, our driver is sternly directed by US soldiers, obviously on high alert, to turn around and take an alternate route. Despite the machine guns, tanks, and the tense, wary soldiers, I bolt from the car, rip off my vest, and throw my helmet to the ground. Ignoring the soldier ordering me to return to the car, I race toward a palm tree, shove down my jeans, then squat and pee as if my life depends on it.

Finished, I rise, compose myself and fix my appearance. I turn around to see the soldiers and my entire convoy laughing. A smile, maybe the first one all day, appears on my face and blossoms into a full-blown laugh. At the very least, my misery is entertaining.

We drive through Baghdad at a snail's pace as US tanks and Humvees are everywhere, at every intersection, creating artificial roadblocks and jamming traffic for miles. I take in the tremendous destruction inflicted by the "shock and awe" bombing campaign. Clearly the objective was met: dramatically and swiftly paralyze and demoralize the enemy. The technology of pinpoint, precision bombs is evident and startling. A building absolutely leveled to its foundation stands next to another totally intact. In this moment, I don't want to think of the lives lost, flesh torn apart, scorched and obliterated in an instant, but there's no way around it. I don't actually see dead bodies, or puddles of blood. I feel them. Men. Women. Children. War. Is this the cost of freedom? Is this the price of eliminating a sadistic, murderous dictator like Saddam Hussein?

Unlike the crowd in Nasiriyah, the Iraqis we pass here seem numb and fatigued. They weave through piles of debris and garbage. Their clothes are stained and dirty. The air reeks of rot and urine and is visibly brown from the dust and smoke.

Looting is rampant. We drive by men who carry bundles of stolen goods wrapped in blankets, while others push makeshift carts that spill over. In the first weeks after Baghdad fell, US troops did not protect public institutions, and consequently schools and hospitals—even the Iraqi National Museum—were looted. Initially it was thought that the looting was spontaneous. When everything around you is falling apart, when you have absolutely no control and the earth is literally trembling beneath your feet, why not take what you can? Later we learned that Hussein and his Ba'athists had directed the looting. It was part of their post-defeat strategy, the killing of Americans soon to follow.

We finally pull up to the Hunting Club, the INC's temporary headquarters and former playground of Uday Hussein, Saddam's eldest son. Surrounded by palm trees, the building itself is fairly nondescript—a long, one-level, brown-brick structure. In stark contrast to the building's drab façade, the air is charged with excitement and even hope. Foreign journalists, Iraqi citizens, tribal chiefs, and secular leaders mix and mingle with INC officials.

Climbing out of the car after our twelve-hour journey, I see my colleague Entifadh Qanbar, the INC's DC-based representative, waiting for me. Our eyes meet and his whole face shines with such an intense pride that a shot of euphoric adrenaline rushes through me. We embrace exuberantly and I realize I am hugging a man who is no longer in exile, a man I've worked side by side with, tirelessly, for months to reach his goal: to stand on the soil of his own country, a free citizen.

"Good thing you're here. We've got work to do!" Entifadh exclaims. "How was the trip in?"

"Uneventful," I lie.

He immediately brings me to see Dr. Chalabi. Noticing me enter the conference room, Chalabi interrupts his meeting, rises, and heads straight for me. As is his style, he extends his hand, foregoing an embrace. His dark, piercing eyes are fixed on mine as he smiles and says, "Thank you for coming, Riva."

"You're welcome, Dr. Chalabi," I respond.

"It was very brave of you," he adds, loud enough for all in the room to hear.

I smile back at him and everyone else, but can't manage any words.

"The new US Administrator for Iraq, Jerry Bremer, has arrived," Chalabi states. "We are now certain that the United States will go to the United Nations and request a Security Council Resolution to declare a formal occupation of Iraq."

My heart sinks, although I knew this decision was likely. The hope of a quick military action to secure the country and an equally quick withdrawal was already disappearing.

"What are the Americans thinking?" Chalabi continues. "Do they not see the effects of Israel's occupation of the Palestinian territories?"

I do not try to answer his question but instead ask what he needs from me now, this man who is my client.

"We are still fighting the decision, and we will need your help. But I feel we will not change the inevitable. As Winston Churchill said, the Americans will settle on the right thing only after exhausting all other options."

With his usual dramatic flair, Chalabi exits the room. I watch him leave and wonder again at the complex motivations that drive this man. He gives nothing away, not even what his ultimate goal may be. I know that in the struggle for power in a country at war, whether Iraq or Liberia, the risks are tremendous for anyone who dreams of winning the game.

EIGHT

PEACE AT LAST

Akosombo, Ghana
Summer, 2003

By the summer of 2003, after years of sounding alarms, appealing to the press and petitioning international authorities for aid and intervention, the anti-Taylor groups in Liberia are finally making real progress. The region's cumulative misery index has become too great for the international community to ignore any longer. Through the tireless advocacy of Ellen, Conmany and many others in Africa, along with the persistence of the US Congress and the bravery of those assigned to the Africa-based Special Court to bring Charles Taylor to justice, there is movement at last. The African regional players, the wider international community and the United States government are finally pulling in the same direction. Charles Taylor's days are numbered.

But as with all things, luck and timing play a key role. This time both are on Liberia's side. As summer wears on, Iraq's descent into post-invasion uncertainty generates a lot of tension between the US and its traditional allies, opening the floodgates for what becomes global criticism of the US and its evaluation of the threat posed by Saddam as well as its ability to meet the post-war challenges and successfully manage an ill-fated occupation.

The wind has shifted. Compared to the increasing quagmire of Iraq, the situation in Liberia now appears to be an opportunity. A mission of mercy in Liberia, with the active participation of the US, will win the support of the global community. Taylor has shown his true colors. The warlord-turned president, in power through a flawed election, six years and tens of thousands of deaths later, is now everyone's bad guy. By intervening even in a limited way in the Liberian crisis, the Bush Administration can now claim unity of purpose, joining an alliance blessed by the Africans and the Europeans, with a clearly delineated UN mandate. In utter contrast to Iraq, Liberia is the perfect consensus mission for the US. It comes with no domestic political costs—that is, as long as the boots of US soldiers do not remain on African soil.

But as the fortunes of Liberia and Ellen now begin to rise, my own fortunes, professionally and personally, take a nosedive. Two journalists for the *Los Angeles Times*, Walter F. Roche Jr. and Ken Silverstein, publish an article about war profiteering around the reconstruction effort in Iraq. And there, in print and circulating around the world digitally, is my name, alongside that of former CIA Director James Woolsey. I am prominently identified as someone who allegedly got rich using "federal funds to drum up prewar support for the Iraqi National Congress." The implication is that I was somehow involved in an effort to deceive the federal government by advocating for the INC, whose own fortunes have fallen sharply in the wake of what now looks like deliberately exaggerated or even wholly invented charges that Saddam possessed weapons of mass destruction. As the situation in Iraq goes south, the press, the public and a lot of US politicians are looking for scapegoats. More news publications pick up the *LA Times* story. My life has turned into a nightmare. I wake up one morning to find myself branded a war profiteer, a willing accomplice in the peddling of false information, a war hawk pushing for the invasion of Iraq, and even someone complicit in the deaths of American soldiers. All the State Department relationships that I built over the years, all of them based on a reputation for trustworthiness and integrity, are suddenly threatened. I did not get proper State Department approval for my convoy into Iraq, that is true. But Chalabi and the INC urged me—begged me, really—to come to Baghdad. I reasoned then that it was a responsibility of my job to be present in Baghdad as the groups met to formulate their next moves. I couldn't afford to wait weeks for State Department approval—even if they were willing to grant it to me.

I am deeply depressed by this turn of events. My spirit is crushed. How can I be so misunderstood? I am the one at BKSH who kept banging away at the importance of representing ethical, inspiring leaders like Ellen. Now I am the bad guy, the loose cannon.

Never since her death have I felt so strongly the need to confide in Oma, to rely on her wisdom and counsel. I long to hear my grandmother's soothing reassurances that all will be well again. I want her to rise up and show them all how wrong they are. I want Oma to tell them who I really am.

◆

Defeat is always difficult to accept. Change is so often frightening. We are reminded by both events that we can never know what the future will bring, what sudden change and unexpected defeats await us.

Shortly after my grandmother passed away, my brothers, sister, cousin and I got together to pack up her personal belongings. Her New York apartment, still under rent control, would be offered up to its first new tenants in over 50 years. Among her things, we found pictures of my grandmother that I never knew existed, pictures from Lithuania and Germany. These were images from a life that she left so abruptly and refused to share with us while she was still alive. "It is just too painful," she would say.

In one of her leather suitcases we found her medical journals in English and in German. Tucked away as a bookmark was the announcement of my college graduation from Tufts University. But more striking was the picture I found of my grandmother and her mother Sophie on holiday, taken during the summer of 1926, somewhere in Europe. My grandmother was so young! Oma was dressed in a light-colored blouse and pleated skirt. She held a sweater in one hand and a walking stick in the other. She had a broad, confident smile on her face, almost like she was laughing. Maybe the photographer made a joke.

Next to my grandmother was her mother, Sophie, wearing a dark-colored, loose fitting dress tightened at the neck and covering up all but her wrists and the tips of her dark leather shoes. Sophie had a mound of white hair arranged in a loose fitting bun. She was the same height as my then-28-year-old grandmother, but she was larger, what one would have described then as a "healthy weight." Sophie too appeared to be laughing, her body almost in motion.

Here were mother and daughter captured forever during a spectacular sunny day in an open field, with hills and a mountain rising behind them. The picture has such depth, you can see the clarity of their faces, the texture of their clothes, the slope of the hills, the cluster of alpine trees reaching toward the snow-covered mountains tops.

I am not certain where the picture was taken. Outside my grandmother's home town of Šiauliai, Lithuania, maybe? Or closer to her adopted city of Berlin? But I do know this. That summer my grandmother had her whole life ahead of her and it must have seemed as sunny and hopeful as that photograph. She would soon graduate from medical school. In December of that year she would wed an aspiring young Jewish doctor who specialized in arthritis, Dr. Jacques Kroner. Her entire family would attend the wedding.

Within a little more than a decade, most of them would be dead.

We can't know the future. Perhaps that is for the best. We push on, hopeful of a better life, eager for sun-filled days spent next to someone we love, blissfully unaware of what the next day might bring.

◆

I am relieved and grateful to turn my attention away from Iraq and begin to focus once again on helping Ellen in Liberia.

Charles Taylor's time is running out. On June 4 the Special Court of Sierra Leone unseals its indictment against Taylor, holding him personally responsible for crimes committed against the people of Sierra Leone. The indictment charges Taylor with a range of atrocities while aiding and abetting the RUF in Sierra Leone. It lays full responsibility at his feet. The action comes with an arrest warrant issued by Interpol for Taylor's immediate extradition. This means that Taylor can no longer travel outside of Liberia without risking arrest and incarceration.

The indictment against Taylor, while a necessary condition to remove him from the political scene in Liberia and discredit him as a leader, is not sufficient. Nor is the increasing advance on Monrovia by an array of armed rebel groups, which is turning Liberia's capital into a war zone and prompting the 13th evacuation of the US mission there, making it the most evacuated US post in the world. To dislodge the cancer that is Charles Taylor will require the words of the US president.

On July 3 on CNN, George W. Bush announces, "Taylor must go," giving the dictator 48 hours to leave Liberia. To the delight of the Liberian people, Bush's words sound like something out of the American Wild West. The president pledges that he will "look at all of the options to determine how best to bring peace and stability" to Liberia, including the possibility of sending troops as part of an international peacekeeping mission. One week later, Bush repeats the same pledge on a Voice of America broadcast.

But those of us familiar with reading between the lines of political statements know that the president has promised nothing specific in that speech. It remains unclear for some time exactly what the US is prepared to do with its own military resources and its diplomatic effort at the United Nations. Still, a blow has been struck, and the Liberian opposition leaders, those who gathered in Ouagadougou one year earlier and are now scattered throughout the continent and the US, know it. Those words by a US president have irreparably damaged Taylor's political support in Liberia, emboldened his armed opponents, and likely taken away the last regional friend he had, with the possible exception of Libya's Muammar Gaddafi. Liberian exiles and others in the Taylor opposition celebrate like the war has ended with President Bush's declaration, although Monrovia remains a battle zone. Says one Liberian friend, "Like when the *Challenger* exploded and the Berlin Wall fell, I will always remember where I was when President Bush said those words, 'Taylor must go!'"

But Taylor, true to form, plays it to the end, publicly suggesting that US internal politics will prevent Bush from responding to the Liberia crisis. "The United States right now," he tells Reuters' David Clarke in an interview in Monrovia on July 10, 2003, "is faced… with the dilemma of committing troops to Liberia, while already having troops all over the world because of the terrible situation in Afghanistan, in Iraq. "And then again, facing an election year soon with the specter of an American boy coming to Liberia and getting hurt is all on his mind, which is right, as president. He ought to think about that."

◆

Ellen, meanwhile, is pleased with Bush's declaration, but she does not feel there is anything yet to celebrate. "It took the US President this long to see what we see?" Ellen asks incredulously. Her attention is now focused on the political situation of a post-Taylor Liberia. "We still have to get the politics right in Liberia," she declares. For Ellen, that means positioning herself to take over the interim administration that will be established.

In early June, 2003, the political theater shifts to Ghana, and the small southern town of Akosombo where the Liberian government, armed rebel groups, including LURD and MODEL, 18 Liberian political partners and leaders from civil society and all of Liberia's fifteen counties are gathered to define a new path forward for Liberia—without Charles Taylor. The negotiations are bolstered by the group Women of Liberia Mass Action for Peace, a movement of non-violent protest that began with thousands of local women praying and singing in a fish market. The group is led by Leymah Gbowee, the Liberian peace activist who will go on to share the Nobel Peace Prize in 2011 with Ellen and Tawakkul Karman of Yemen. Their movement will later includes a highly-publicized sex strike and the threat of a curse. Many of these women will form a significant group of supporters for Ellen. They provide the human interest backdrop for the meetings, hosted by Ghanaian President John Kufuor. Accra becomes the new battleground and center stage for deciding the future of Liberia.

In many ways, the structure of the Accra meetings is not different from what Conmany and Ellen managed in Ougadougou. Much of the framework of the Accra Comprehensive Peace Agreement is drawn from the Ougadougou Accords. The distinction of Accra now is that the armed movements are at the table, and unannounced to the civilian leaders, will ultimately wield the decisive power in defining a post-Taylor program. The new comprehensive peace accords are to lay the foundation for the country's return to democratic government in October 2005. Until that time a two-year transitional government will lead the country forward. The Accra peace accords also call for a more robust and neutral peace-keeping force under the auspices of the United Nations the United Nations Mission in Liberia, or UNMIL—that will not play politics and will provide real security and the political freedom necessary for the Liberian people to choose their next generation of leaders.

Ellen is now determined to take leadership of the emerging interim administration that will govern Liberia. Many Liberians in the struggle convince her that this period will be "a determinant," that "Liberia's future rested upon it." But neither I nor the other friends who have fought with Ellen feel that it is a wise political decision to aim for the leadership of the temporary government.

"Why not wait the two years," I ask. "An open and transparent election is the only way you'll gain the validation you want."

But Ellen is insistent. Her close friend and colleague Conmany Wessah says to me, "You need to understand where Ellen is coming from. How many years has she fought this fight? She's been challenging the system since the late 1970s. It is something she can see and feel now." Then he adds, "Ellen knows she is getting older. There might not be another chance."

I understand all that, I reassure him. I still disagree. It is not her destiny to play caretaker. I feel that I know this intrinsically. Still, I am not in a position to judge Ellen's choices. "Look at your own," Ellen will retort.

Eleven candidates are to submit to an open vote of the delegates. Ellen asks if I will work with our friends in Congress and the State Department so that Washington will send "signals" to the delegates, showing that Ellen has the support of the United States, that she is the preferred candidate. In Washington parlance, this means statements of support without direct US government attribution. Despite my reservations, I give it my best effort, reaching out to the US Assistant Secretary of State and to other contacts in the State Department, the White House and in Congress. But I receive nothing beyond the familiar reluctance of US officials to "take sides in what is inherently a Liberian political process." I understand from a theoretical standpoint, but I find that insular attitude so ironic and detached, given how much money is changing hands in the halls of Akosombo to buy votes and allegiances.

When Ellen asks me for a status report, I tell her straight that when asked, US officials are likely to note her leadership capability and her record in Liberia's struggle. But they will not show a political preference to those in Akosombo.

In the end, though, it doesn't really matter how aggressively the US petitions for Ellen. The armed groups—which include a faction of Taylor loyalists—move in a block, and announce that they will have the final say in determining the interim leader. This, they claim, is their right, due to their control on the ground. True peace, they declare, can only come with their collaboration. They will choose among the three top vote-getters, Rudolph Sherman, chairman of the True Whig Party, Liberia's oldest political party, Charles Gyude Bryant, a member of the same LAP that had precipitously withdrawn its support for Ellen in 1997, and Ellen. Even though Ellen wins a majority of the delegates, it becomes clear that the Taylor faction will not let her to assume the leadership post. They know that she will exercise independence and pursue an aggressive stabilization agenda that will leave no room for private deals and hidden agreements among those vying for power. Taylor himself issues borderline threats. "Ellen Johnson Sirleaf leading a transition government?" he says to Reuters' correspondent David Clarke, "The war would never stop. If I ever thought that someone was trying to fashion a system where these failed politicians that participated in the elections, that did not win, would come here to head a government, I would not step out of this country."

Stopping the war is the first order of business for the regional players. Holding a true democratic vote can come later. Ellen loses the regional African block due to Taylor's public and behind-the-scenes lobbying. On August 21, Charles Gyude Bryant is chosen as Chair of the National Transitional Government of Liberia (NTGL), effective October 14. This paves the way for the *Economic Community Of West African States* (ECOWAS) peacekeeping mission to expand into a 3,600-strong multinational force, drawn from Benin, Gambia, Ghana, Guinea-Bissau, Mali, Nigeria, Senegal and Togo.

Ten days prior, Taylor leaves Liberia for temporary exile in Nigeria. The US, while not committing any forces on the ground, stations three war ships and a Marine expeditionary force of 2,300 personnel off the Liberian coast and flies US helicopters over Monrovia to show its military presence. It is a clear victory for the Bush Administration in its international diplomacy. The night prior to his departure, in a rambling address on national television, Taylor tells the country, "History will be kind to me. I have fulfilled my duties." (Nicle Itanao, *Christian Science Monitor*, August 12, 2003.).

"Again, there was no democracy in the Liberian vote," protests Ellen when she calls me with the results. She was right of course, but I was relieved more than disappointed. "I am sorry, Ellen," I say, "I know it was not a fair fight. But maybe it is all for the best." Ellen is silent. She returns to the line, her voice raised, almost in anger. "Riva, do not ever tell me what is best for the Liberian people!"

Though I cannot be sure, and I never asked, particularly after that last exchange, I cannot help but wonder if Ellen too might ultimately have been relieved that it was Gyude Bryant who was selected as chair of the NTGL, and not her. The more we learned about the process, the clearer it became that the interim leader of Liberia had been dealt a compromised hand, placed in charge of a government he did not control, with officials who owed him no loyalty and a national budget that required several signatures beyond his own.

The best way forward now, it seems, is for Ellen to return to Liberia, contribute to the transition, but not bear the full weight of this temporary government. When Bryant asks her to take the position as head of the Governance Reform Commission, she agrees.

On December 20 of that year, Ellen writes,

Dear All: As you know, for the past five years I have been based in Abidjan, Côte d'Ivoire representing our consulting firm and carrying out my professional and political activities from this base.

Now that we have a welcomed political change in Liberia and I have committed to support the transitional process, which is underway. I have decided to relocate to home permanently and to close our operations in Côte d'Ivoire as of Tuesday, 23 December 2003. Unfortunately, most services in Liberia have been inoperative for the past several years and it will take some time for the Transitional Government to get them restored. In the meanwhile, I can be reached, wherever and whenever possible, at unitylady2003@yahoo. com...

When I read Ellen's email address, I know what our campaign slogan will be in two years: unitylady2005.

Ellen walking with team to Unity Party Conference Center, Montserrado County, Liberia, July 2005.

NINE

SHE'S GOING TO WIN

Dulles Airport
Spring, 2005

With Ellen's return to Liberia to assume her position in the interim government, I return to my other duties at BKSH. My goal is to keep my head down, concentrate on my work, and stay out of the spotlight. I wake up every morning dreading yet another Google alert blaming me or my company for everything that has gone wrong in Iraq, from the botched intelligence on weapons of mass destruction to the insidious corruption in the Iraqi contracting process, to the deaths of American servicemen and women. Googling *Riva Levinson + pictures* punches up an array of images, including a lurid cartoon of President George W. Bush having sex with Saddam Hussein, titled, "the screwing of America."

As the war in Iraq drags on, the fortunes of the Iraqi National Congress fade. In May 2004 Ahmed Chalabi suffers the indignity of being held at gunpoint as his offices are raided by the US military. The Pentagon stops its funding of the INC. Chalabi soon re-emerges as an outspoken critic of the US occupation and allies himself with anti-American factions, but in the uncertain world of Iraqi politics, it is too little, too late. When elections are held in December 2005, the INC fails to win even a single seat in the new national congress. In November of 2015, at the age of 71, Chalabi died of a sudden heart attack. The Iraqi government honored his service to the nation with a State funeral. Chalabi was buried in Imam Musa Kadhim holy shrine. The global media documented his passing with headlines, such as "The death of the man who drove the US to war." *(France24, November 3, 2015)*

My portfolio of clients has stabilized over the months since my convoy into Iraq and I use that work to restore my reputation and my emotional balance. As usual, my work in Africa proves to be the most fulfilling. The effort that I began in Côte d'Ivoire with Western Wireless has won me a reputation as a fierce advocate for commercial disputes in challenging locales. Ellen was right, the enemies you accumulate along the way constitute a badge of honor. Slowly I am returning from my professional and personal low point.

On February 7, 2005, the National Electoral Commission of Liberia sets the date for Liberia's presidential and legislative elections: October 11, 2005, eight months away. Imagine my elation when, standing in line for a noontime sandwich at Subway on L Street, my phone rings and on the line is the familiar crackle and buzz of a long-distance call from Liberia. It is Ellen, calling me from her home in Monrovia.

"I am running for president," she declares in her familiar, determined voice. "Are you in?"

I can hardly believe it.

I am beyond happy. Does Ellen realize how depressed I have been, given the developments in Iraq? Does she understand that with this one gesture she has restored my sense of purpose and stopped me from feeling so pathetically sorry for myself? Does she appreciate that at this moment in my professional life, when everyone else is piling on, almost for sport, that she is one of the few people to look past the headlines, straight into me, with no doubts, no reservations? I don't think she fathoms that it is her approval that matters most to me.

Forget Iraq. Here is a chance to show the world what the future of Africa can look like if the right kind of leader steps forward and is chosen in a fair and open election.

"I am *all* in!" I scream. The Subway customers and staff, alarmed, turn to stare at me. I give them a sheepish grin and a "thumbs up."

"This time," Ellen continues, "we will need you on the ground here, as well as in Washington. Can you do that? Will your company give you that flexibility?"

"One hundred percent yes!" I reply, with a little more control this time. I will worry about the details later. I know the struggle that awaits me, convincing my company to let me take on an assignment that is not likely to bring in even pocket change, at least in the near-term. I can hear them already. "Sirleaf? She's running? Again?" My response will be, "Damn right." The only difference this time is: she's going to win.

◆

Within a few weeks I have secured the proper permissions and arranged my work schedule. But my earlier bravado has shrunk from a shout to a whimper. I soon realize just how far behind we are in the perceptions game. It is as if our opponents have already dashed out of the starting blocks and we are still on our knees, tying our running shoes. Piles of money are already being spent by the top male candidates, including charismatic former soccer superstar, George Weah, and the experienced, longtime Liberian political leader, Charles Brumskine. Ellen has the impressive international credentials, her central role in the long Liberian struggle, and her place at the forefront of the national campaign for peace. But this is Africa. The men have one simple and powerful advantage. They are men. In a traditionally male-dominated field such as politics, a 66-year-old grandmother is not even on a level playing field. She has to fight to get on the field at all. It is all too clear at the outset of Ellen's campaign why, in the modern history of the continent, there has never been an elected female leader of any country.

From where we stand in March, it does not look like Ellen has any chance to break the pattern. Charles Brumskine has already landed a cover story in the *Washington Post Magazine* titled, "The Man Who Would Be President." And George Weah, already enjoying rock-star status as a national soccer idol, will be the subject of an article in next month's *New York Times Magazine*. The title, we are told, will be "King George."

While it is true that most Liberians don't read the *Post* or the *Times*, international media coverage matters in Liberia. I can already see the campaign managers for Weah and Brumskine distributing their US articles as endorsements by the American media. As if the predictability of the American press were not enough to deal with, we also have to contend with the American government and its lack of imagination. After a few visits to the State Department and the National Security Council, followed by an excursion to the McLean Family Diner, off Route 123 in downtown McLean, for an off-the-record meeting with friends at the CIA, I can see that the conventional wisdom has already been passed down among Washington insiders: *Ellen Johnson Sirleaf has no chance of being elected president of Liberia.* As one CIA contact states matter-of-factly, "There is no way that Ellen can top the allure of a soccer superstar, even if he only has an eighth-grade education." An official at the State Department's Bureau of African Affairs sums it up neatly. "She is a woman. In the context of African politics, that's three strikes against her right there." Besides, adds the State official, twisting the knife, "Sirleaf is just too old. Liberia needs a fresh face."

An even more damaging assessment comes from an official based at the US embassy in Monrovia. "Ellen is too combative. She is promising to discard GEMAP if she wins." GEMAP, the Governance Economic Management and Assistance Program, was established to provide international oversight to combat the entrenched corruption in Liberian government. "Liberians are not ready to govern on their own," an official lectured me. "There is no institutional capacity. George Weah understands that."

I assume that this criticism of Ellen is being delivered through me because no one has the guts to deliver it to Ellen directly. Which is smart, I reflect. I wouldn't want to be in that meeting.

I argue back. Ellen, I point out, can capture the vote of the women of Liberia, more than 50 percent of the electorate. She has a chance to make history and become the first woman to lead an African nation. There is no better steward of Liberia's future, I point out, than Ellen Johnson Sirleaf, and the US government would be wise to do everything it can to support Ellen.

But now in 2005, just as in 1997 and 2003, I get the same answer. "We don't take sides in a political contest. It is up to the Liberian people to decide."

"Do you really think anyone else plays by those rules?" I want to ask them. But I ask it only silently, and only to myself.

◆

So what do you do when the Bush Administration shuts you down? You go to Congress. And when the major US media has already made up its mind? You target the African and the European press. And when campaigns are being run like they have always been—persuasion through money, with loyalties being bought and sold? You go directly to the Liberian people. You conduct a poll. You base your message and build your campaign upon a real understanding of your electorate. Finally, what do you do when there is no way you can beat a Liberian soccer legend on the first round of an election that requires a majority of 50 percent? You don't even try. You shoot for the second spot, and assume that in a crowded field George Weah will only get a plurality. Then you target all those who voted against him – the voters who make up the majority.

◆

I agree with Ellen that I cannot advocate for her effectively without witnessing her campaign in person, seeing the energy and enthusiasm around her candidacy, and being able to report back to official Washington, with authority, that she can win. I need to be in Liberia. In eight years of working with Ellen, from 1997 to 2005, I never made it to Liberia. During the 1997 presidential campaign, I was five months pregnant, so travel was impossible then. When the security situation stabilized in 2003 following the Accra peace accords, I had no mandate and no budget. I have extensive experience in Africa, of course, from Angola to Namibia to South Africa to Côte d'Ivoire and beyond. Now at last I am going to Liberia. Finally! I am excited. I am nervous. I am worried that I will not meet Ellen's expectations. Am I really ready for this, after all? It does not help my self-confidence to be introduced to someone named Amara Konneh.

Amara is a member of the Liberian diaspora and is currently a network engineer for a group based in Philadelphia. Ellen told me that he will be my partner now in my work on her campaign effort. We are to travel together. Amara and I arrange to meet in early April at my offices on K Street.

Amara fled Liberia during the war after his uncle was killed by Taylor's men. He spent nearly three years in a refugee camp on the Guinea side of the border where he was later identified by the International Committee of the Red Cross as having exceptional talent. They eventually helped him get to the United States for schooling. Amara was granted political asylum in 1993. Like almost every Liberian I have come to know, Amara has a story of struggle and deprivation and perseverance. He does not know Ellen personally, but is committed to her candidacy and the possibilities of Liberia under her leadership. He refers to her as Mrs. Sirleaf. Amara is thirty-five, bespectacled, boyishly handsome.

Also at the meeting is Abdoulye Dukulé, Duke to some, the Professor to others. He is laid-back in style. It is almost impossible to imagine him in a necktie. Duke is one of Liberia's most well-respected journalists, and he has a doctorate in filmmaking. Founder of the *Perspective (of Liberia)*, the country's first online news journal, Duke met Ellen while interviewing her for one of the *Perspective's* very first articles in 2001. He has been a committed supporter since. He facilitates the meeting between Amara and me, and he seems to be expecting things to unfold badly.

Sipping coffee in our small conference room surrounded by historical pictures of Washington, DC, I can tell that Amara is not convinced that I can offer anything worthwhile to Ellen. I understand his skepticism. He doesn't know my background. I am not Liberian. I don't know the terrain. To him I am just some random hire from some K Street lobbying firm. I can see the wisdom in Ellen's thinking: a smart, young Liberian exile to give our US effort some authenticity. But still I feel let down. Doesn't she trust me to do the work? Why do I need Amara?

Our entire first meeting in early April is an exercise in second-guessing. I propose a campaign slogan for consideration. *Ellen will make the country work; she will put you to work.* "What do you think, Amara?" I ask.

Amara takes the opportunity to school me. "Unlike in the United States," he informs me, "Liberians don't believe that they will get paid after working. Most Liberians right now are actually working but getting no wages in return."

"Okay," I say, moving on. "I will put together a strategic framework for the campaign, incorporating the best tactics I have seen in the US and other projects around the world, including South Africa's first all-race election. What do you think?" I am trying to make my comeback with Amara.

I look towards Duke, who has said very little during our discussion. My eyes plead with him for some sign of agreement, a nod of the head. He just shrugs his shoulders.

Amara pauses and then replies, "I have put together a small group of Liberian professionals to do some strategic thinking on how best to structure Ellen's campaign. We are meeting again this Saturday in Pennsylvania. Why don't you start there?"

When he sees my disappointment after he has dismissed another of my suggestions, he adds quickly, "It was just an idea."

Like it or not, I think to myself, we will travel to Liberia together—me for the very first time, and for Amara, his first trip back since fleeing Liberia as a teenage boy. The collaboration has not gotten off to the greatest of starts.

It is afternoon rush hour, Monday, July 11, and as usual I arrive early at my gate for the United Airlines flight to Brussels, where we will then connect to the semi-weekly Brussels Airlines flight to Monrovia. It is the only sure way of getting to Liberia, a route kept open to accommodate the thousands of UN peacekeepers and humanitarian workers.

It is past the boarding time and passengers are already seated on our flight. But there is no sign of Amara.

"Where are you, Amara?" I shout into my cell phone. "They've already called our row number for boarding!"

"I am here, on the Beltway," answers Amara. He sounds a lot less self-assured. "I am trying to get to the Dulles access road. My wife decided to drive me from Philly. I feel like we are doing laps now!"

"It's a right-hand exit just before Tyson's Corner, if you miss it again, you'll miss the flight," I warn him.

Twenty minutes later every passenger on the flight has boarded. I am the only person standing in the way of the ramp closing. I beg the United Flight attendant to wait just one more minute. She is ready to call Security.

"This is about the future of Liberia," I plead. "Our mission is essential to the peace of an entire nation!" I am trying to reason with a very disinterested young woman with very blond hair and an impressive dose of eye makeup. She is rapidly losing patience with me. I am panicked, knowing that if we miss this flight we miss our only window to get out on the campaign trail with Ellen. I can't let that happen. In seconds I will have to make a decision whether to abandon Amara and go to Monrovia on my own.

"Are you getting on this airplane or not, ma'am?" asks the woman for what certainly will be the final time.

Just then I spot Amara bolting through the Terminal, completely out of breath, his canary-yellow and royal-blue Ralph Lauren polo shirt, likely bought just for this occasion, soaked with perspiration. His close shaven head glistens with beads of sweat that drip down his face, making it appear as if he were crying.

Not a bad idea, I think. Contrition.

The blonde woman takes the opportunity to scold the breathless Amara. "This lady here wouldn't let the plane take off! We would have already left if she wasn't so insistent. You owe her one."

That was unexpected, but it is always nice to be appreciated. We board the plane to a round of applause from the flight crew and passengers. Within minutes we are in the air, on our way to Liberia. What awaits us is either a chance to be part of history, or—I pray silently that it will not come to pass—the final, crushing defeat of a true hero.

TEN

BEING THERE

Monrovia, Liberia
July, 2005

L iberia in July is heavy with humidity. The air is like a warm, moist
blanket. Your clothes feel damp the moment you walk off the plane
and they never seem to dry again. Liberia averages some of the highest
annual rainfall in the world. The next thing that hits your senses is the
smell of things burning. It is everywhere, in the streets, in the buildings,
and even in the homes. Wood, charcoal, and anything else that will burn
are the primary sources of energy for most Liberians, even in Monrovia,
the capital.

I've just arrived and I am melting. I have been engulfed in the vapors
of a hybrid barbeque with Amara in tow.

I see the name "Reeva" hand-written on a scrap of paper. It is Amara's
first time back as an adult and I am ushering him through the crowd as
it swarms around us.

After struggling to hold onto our bags while strangers keep trying to
"help" us, we climb into the waiting vehicle as the day goes dark and we
pull onto the road heading left toward the capital. I then realize just how
remote Robertsfield is from downtown Monrovia. Not built for civilian
air traffic, Robertsfield was initially constructed to accommodate US
military aircraft on the African continent during World War II. As a
convenient consequence, it has one of the longest runways in Africa, and
by design, conceived to be inaccessible to the local population.

On the way into town it hits me, literally, just how bad the roads still
are. In the pitch black, the potholes become invisible horrors, as the tires
dip and the car's underbelly scrapes the gravel. With each explosive jolt I

wish more that the seatbelts worked. I close my eyes and hope to absorb the thump, thump of the abused tires.

Two hours later, Amara and I are finally dropped at our hotel, the Urban Villa, slightly rattled but whole and happy. The Villa is located on Tubman Boulevard in the Sinkor section of Monrovia, a few blocks from the long South Atlantic shoreline. It is now after midnight. The diesel-fired pump lacks the power, at night, to push water all the way up to my room on the second floor, and the shower I crave doesn't happen until dawn.

The next morning, maneuvering through the streets of Monrovia in our SUV, I am struck with the daunting task that lay ahead for the country. The roads are barely passable. Telephone poles have been cut down for fuel, and streetlights stripped of metal, wiring, and bulbs. The corrugated iron roofs on neighborhood schools were ripped off long ago to build makeshift shelters. There is no electricity, no sewers or sanitation, and in most dwellings and buildings, no running water.

There are, however, cell phones. They are everywhere. Charles Taylor has seen to that. Rumor has it that even in exile in Nigeria he still receives 60 cents on every dollar made through Lone Star Communications, one of Liberia's few cell providers. Vendors sell pre-paid phone cards on every street corner at almost any time, day or night. The cards are sold along with local baked goods, bananas, mangos, and homemade soaps. Liberians can phone their relatives in the United States some 4600 miles away, but they can't get water from a faucet.

Although the infrastructure is crumbling, in the streets you can still feel an indomitable spirit at work. Everyone I observe is in a state of great anticipation. It's as if the whole country has just heaved a collective sigh of relief, a long exhale. The State Department guidance to American citizens has got it all wrong, I think, making it sound as if visitors to Liberia are under siege: *Don't go out at night. Don't go to public gatherings. Stay away from campaign rallies. Be aware of your surroundings…* They might have advised Americans just to stay home. But after nearly 20 years of traveling the continent, I know how telling vibes can be. And here in Monrovia I feel a vibe of joy and hope that we need to connect to Ellen's campaign.

♦

Ellen's house is just off of Tubman Boulevard in Monrovia, a kilometer or so from the beach, just far enough from the main road to provide a perimeter of security for her small staff to police. The house is a modest two-story home, white cinderblock, with four bedrooms, a single sitting area, dining room and kitchen. Food always seems to be cooking in the kitchen, with dozens of people milling about. A single generator powers the house, offering up electricity in the evening hours. When we arrive for breakfast that morning, I am surprised by the figure that greets me. I barely recognize Ellen. She is wearing jeans—I have never seen her in anything but formal western business attire or the traditional Liberian long skirt—and a Unity Party campaign T-shirt. She wears knee-high muck boots. Her attire seems to say that she is ready for the hard, dirty work of a political campaign. She greets us warmly. She is so pleased to see us both in Liberia! We are offered a traditional breakfast of yams and stewed fish. I note that Ellen chooses oatmeal.

After breakfast we get straight to work. Amara, Ellen and I go through the itinerary for the next three days. Amara and I will meet with Ellen's top campaign officials, including her campaign chairman, the aptly named Willis Knuckles, back then a trusted and valued advisor. (Knuckles will later suffer acute embarrassment when nude photos of him surface in 2007, showing him in compromising positions with two women. These make the front pages of most of Liberia's newspapers and force his retirement from public life, at least for a time. Whether or not he has been set up makes little difference; the damage is done). The plan is that we will go with Ellen to various campaign events, including a discussion with students at the University of Liberia. The next day we will attend her rally on the outskirts of Monrovia at the Unity Party Conference Center. The third day we will go over our observations with the party leadership and begin to shape a plan to move forward.

Amara and I discover that we are joining a team already in place. There is the Unity Party leadership that speaks with certainty about the right path to victory. There is a political operative from Baltimore named Larry Gibson who has already defined how Ellen will be presented in the campaign posters and other materials. Amara and I know that we will have to be selective with advice and realistic about what kind of impact we can have on a political apparatus that is already up and running. For Amara, it is all about data. He is convinced that no one really understands the Liberian electorate. Polling, he believes, however rudimentary, will reveal the base emotion that we can to tap into. If we can capture that and incorporate it into the campaign message, it could very well enable Ellen to break through. I recall that in the Taylor election of 1997, the driver of the electorate was fear—fear of what he would do if he did not win. I am convinced that fear will not determine this election. But what will be the driver this time?

For me, it is something less tangible than data. "We need people to believe," I tell Amara. "We need them to see the possibilities that we do, to realize Ellen's potential. We need people to believe that Ellen has a chance, that history can be made in Liberia. We start there. That's the base point we need to establish so we can track our momentum."

Amara and I travel with Ellen to her various campaign stops in Montserrado County. At the University of Liberia, hundreds of students squeeze into a makeshift auditorium, fighting for space to hear Ellen speak. She captures their attention right away and they listen without interruption. The Q&A is not so orderly. For the students, it is all about *their* education, about *their* future. But the important thing is that they all want to have their voices heard by Ellen, a clear sign that they believe she can and will actually do something about their concerns.

"What would you do to improve the university conditions?"

"What about new technologies? We are falling behind in the world."

"What about the quality of our teachers?"

"What would your international friends do to help us?"

Amara is pleased. "This is a good and informal focus group. We need to do more of these."

The next day we head to the Unity Party Conference Center about 30 kilometers outside Monrovia. It is likely to be one of her largest campaign rallies to date. Thousands of supporters are expected to pack the hall, many of them women. We are increasingly convinced that this is Ellen's core constituency—as long as the women register to vote in numbers equal to their male counterparts—which unfortunately is not trending anywhere in Africa.

Ellen's advance security reports that the Unity Party Conference Center is filled to capacity and that the warm-up political acts, candidates for the senate and legislature of Montserrado County, are keeping the crowd energized, waiting for Ellen's arrival. About one mile from the Center, Ellen orders the convoy to stop. But aren't we more than an hour late, I wonder?

"I do not want to pull up in a motorcade," announces Ellen. "It signals that I deserve better than those inside. Let us get out and walk."

So we do. We all get out of our vehicles and walk a mile down the dirt road, in the pouring rain, generating an impromptu parade of followers along the way. When word reaches the conference hall that Ellen is arriving on foot, her supporters flow out to escort her. About a hundred yards from the Center, the two crowds merge into one. In the rain, chanting, singing, horns blasting, hundreds of us walk up the steps to Unity Party Hall and make a loud, triumphant, high-energy entrance. It is an impressive sight. We believe it to be a sign of things to come. If we are going to change history, we might already have started, right here.

Amara and I have arranged to meet a *London Times* journalist, Prue Clarke, at the venue. She is the only prominent journalist we can convince to come to observe the event and interview Ellen. Everyone else, including journalists for *Voice of America, Associated Press* and local stringers for the *Washington Post* and the *Christian Science Monitor*, are on the campaign trail with "King George." Even Clarke hedges her bets and seeks to manage expectations with us, as she writes in an email.

I hope to catch a few moments of Ellen's time while I'm there. The focus on the story will be Weah—his international fame makes him of interest to my editor. But I would like to include Ellen, her plans for Liberia and her criticism of Weah's plans, if she is willing.

Clarke is on site to witness Ellen's entrance and the crowd's overwhelming enthusiasm for her. It is tough to get a read on what any reporter is thinking, but it feels to us that Clarke knows she is watching something special happening. Her interview includes exactly the questions we hoped for, ones we could have written ourselves, such as "Does

Ellen believe that she is poised to make history as the first female elected head of state on the African continent?"

◆

As planned, we close our trip in meetings with Ellen's campaign team to provide our observations and recommendations. I focus my advice on the need for discipline and structure, singling out the messages that resonated and making sure that they are echoed through all party surrogates. I also remind everyone that at the end of the day it only matters if our supporters are registered to vote, and only then if they make it to the polls. What is the plan to make that happen?

Again, for Amara, it remains all about data—the importance of conducting a poll in all fifteen counties, how that might be done using those passionate students from the University of Liberia deployed throughout the country with a basic questionnaire. He emphasizes how this data will be critical to the allocation of scarce campaign resources. Although there is a lot of nodding heads, it is difficult to know if our recommendations really penetrate. But we know what we need to do upon our return to DC.

Riva with Amara Konneh, journalist Prue Clarke, and Liberian journalist, July 2005.

ELEVEN

ELLEN, SHE'S OUR MAN!

Monrovia, Liberia
Fall, 2005

On Saturday, July 30, in a front-page article for the *London Times*, Prue Clarke publishes her story. As she promised, it is largely about George Weah. Could he successfully move from soccer stardom to the Liberian presidency? But within the article, punched out in bold letters, highlighted and showcased in the margin, is this pull quote:

"With or without Mr. Weah, the election promises to make history. The second in this two-horse race is Ellen Johnson Sirleaf, 70, a Harvard-trained political stalwart who, should she win, will be the first woman to lead a modern African nation."

Clarke got Ellen's age wrong; she is 66, not 70. Amara and I let it go; Ellen not so easily.

Clarke writes almost apologetically to Amara and me when she emails the article to us:

I don't understand why there's not more interest in the first credible woman candidate as leader of an African nation. If she wins, the media will come running. Cheers and good luck, Prue.

It isn't the front-page article we wanted, and it isn't even a story focused on Ellen. But it is enough for us to circulate widely to potential advocates and supporters and to reprint on campaign flyers in several local dialects. As in any campaign, whether in the first world or developing world, it's all about momentum, who has it, who doesn't. The money, the donations, the tangible support, the physical presence at rallies as well as the willingness to sport party colors and paraphernalia and to openly associate oneself with the candidate—all of that only comes when people believe that you have a chance to win, and that their support matters. In June Ellen was ranked a generous fifth in a pool of 22 candidates. Now, a month later, the perception is that Ellen Johnson Sirleaf is mounting a serious challenge to the leader, soccer star "King" George Weah.

I call Ellen in Monrovia. "I can do a lot with this," I report to her, referring to Clarke's shout-out.

"We need others of prominence to create an echo effect and a sense of inevitability," Ellen sums up neatly. As usual, she is right.

"I will turn to our friends in Congress and to some of the major media houses," I tell Ellen. "Let's see if we can get them to recognize the historical significance of your candidacy." I ask about Amara and his hopes for gathering more data. "Have you reviewed his proposal for funding? He needs to be with you in Liberia."

There is a pause and Ellen explains, "The campaign team has not prioritized his interventions. They believe money is better spent on traditional rallies."

Even though Ellen knows how important Amara's contribution will be to our election effort, she also knows that she cannot upset the party apparatus that she largely inherited and that needs to remain upbeat and fully committed to her. But I know that we also need what Amara can provide. There has to be a way.

"Ellen, let me talk to our friends here. I think I have an idea", I tell her.

I decide to call Brad Horwitz, the president of Western Wireless—and now my client, thanks to Ellen.

"Hey Brad," I announce, trying to sound sunny and cheerful. I know that I am waking him up. It is 5:45 a.m. in Seattle. "How would you like to be part of history?"

"Whose history and for what purpose?" he responds grumpily.

I explain to him about Amara and his plans for in-country polling, how decisive a role that kind of modern data collection can play in the campaign. "Brad, what do you think? How would you like to fund this effort? The Liberian diaspora in the United States has mobilized in support of Ellen. Can I put you in touch with their head?"

There is silence on the line, then a long sigh and a mumbled promise that he will "mull it over." It is a record-fast mulling. Ten minutes later I get a one-line email: *Just get me the instructions. BJH*

By the end of the week, Amara has the necessary funds to fly back to Liberia and mobilize his 25-plus university students and dispatch them to the market centers in six of Liberia's most populous counties. Amara has so many students volunteer to participate that he can't accommodate them all. We take that as another positive sign.

The polling plan and the field questionnaire are sketched-out on the back of a napkin from Sam's Barbeque, the rib shack near Ellen's home, a regular stop for the team as the place never seems to close. Those vying for space on that napkin include Amara, Duke, Medina Wesseh, (Conmany's wife), and Morris Dukuly.

At the grassroots level, this campaign is beginning to look stronger. Do we dare to use the words *gaining momentum*?

Amara completes his fieldwork by the end of August. In early September his analysis of the data is complete. Just as he promised, we now possess a definitive road map that indicates which counties merit increased resources and manpower. The data confirm what we all suspected: Ellen cannot beat George Weah in the first round. No one can. We need to focus solely on surging ahead of Charles Brumskine, who continues to run neck-and-neck with us in the national polls. We need to capture the second spot and make it to the run-off.

But the data from Amara's polling also reveals something even more important to us—something that turns out to be the breakthrough play, the element that makes all the difference. The survey participants tell us that for them, this election must be grounded in hope for the future. The single most important issue for the Liberian voters is access to education for their children. What they want above all else is that their children have the chance to live better lives.

There it is. Our key message, our goal, our focus. We share the findings with Ellen, and the campaign incorporates the more focused message into all of her speeches and adapts this fine-tuned talking point for her surrogates. And it begins to work. By mid-September we can sense the electorate shift toward Ellen. We can see it in the growing numbers at her rallies and in the enthusiasm of the crowds. In the marketplace, hundreds of women strip pieces of Ellen's posters off the cement walls and fasten those shreds to their clothing to be identified with her. Even the local and international media begin now to follow Ellen on the campaign trail. Ellen—the woman who might just make history. Now when Amara sifts through the new polling data, what he sees thrills us and lifts our spirits: Ellen is climbing toward the lead.

"Ellen, She's our Man!" This slogan becomes the rallying cry as we enter the final weeks of the campaign. Brilliant. I wish that I could take credit for it, but it just seemed to appear out of nowhere.

Then from Washington, DC, an influential member of Congress puts herself on the line for Ellen. Congresswoman Diane Watson (D-CA), a member of the House Subcommittee on Africa and International Human Rights, issues a statement on October 3 stating that Ellen's victory "could usher in an era of empowerment for women on the continent." She further praises Ellen for "running on a reform, anti-corruption agenda, which threatens to upset the established political order not only in Liberia but also in Africa at large." *The Liberian Daily Observer* reports the next day, "Ellen Receives Massive International Endorsement!"

On October 11, 2005, the first round of voting takes place. There are 22 candidates. I am in DC and there is nothing I can do but wait. It is excruciating. "We won't know anything for several days, Riva," Amara reassures me with some annoyance in his voice. "I promise, you will be my first phone call, even before I call my wife!" He then stops taking my calls.

It is not until four days later, October 15, when the official results of the first-round voting start coming in from the National Electoral Commission. And, as promised, I am Amara's first call.

"It's between us and Weah!" Amara shouts at me.

It is remarkable how close the results resemble Amara's polling sample of 2,000 national voters. Weah, as expected, finishes first with 28.3 percent, but he is far short of a majority. In second place, "after a remarkable climb from the middle of the pack," is Ellen Johnson Sirleaf with

19.8 percent. Seventy-four percent of the country's eligible voters cast ballots. The first-round results elevate Amara in the eyes of everyone on the campaign team, including the old guard who did not trust analytical demographics. Amara will now define the strategy for the second round to be held on November 8.

I listen impatiently to the number crunching.

"Now that Ellen has won the first round, we need to create a sense of inevitability," says Amara. "How can you help from DC?"

I hesitate for several seconds, running the touch points through my head, "I know exactly where to go," I tell Amara assertively.

A few days after Amara's call, I set up another off-the-record breakfast meeting at the McLean Family Diner with my "agency contacts," as I call them. Over weak coffee and scrambled eggs, I open my manila folder and go through the first-round election results from the National Elections Commission and our internal polling. I then share our assumptions that the majority of voters decided *against* Weah, and that we have a strategy to capture a majority of the vote.

"We have a decisive path to victory," I say with confidence. I suggest they consider changing their predictive modeling, unless they want to end up being flat-out wrong and look hopelessly bad. I have given them a chance to get it right. If they go for it, then they just might help me create the reality that I *am* right. I can see them wavering. While there will be no article, no statement, no public prediction, the new internal analysis that they share within the inner circles of the US government will have more impact than any public statement.

Ellen's team deploys now with renewed confidence. Our plan is unfolding perfectly. The majority of people voted against Weah, as we predicted. Those voters become our first priority. On the campaign trail, at rallies and events, Ellen continues to hit hard on her themes of education and the future, delivering a message of optimism. She is buoyant. And the crowds are large, loud and energized. "Iron Lady goes for Gold," the *Washington Post* emblematically runs as a news headline.

Weah's team now seems deflated. In their minds, they saw their candidate as inevitable. Everyone told them so, including the US government and the international media. Weah and his people are caught by surprise. They didn't plan for the long game, and there is no time to recover.

We are delighted but not surprised when Weah opts out of a planned second-round debate. It is taken as a sign of weakness, which it is. One-on-one, the soccer star with an eighth-grade education is no match for the Harvard-educated former finance minister. Ducking the debate is also a serious strategic mistake, as Weah loses the opportunity to get on UN radio nationwide. Soon thereafter his campaign managers get desperate. They begin to issue vague threats about what will happen if the election is "stolen" from him.

On November 8, Liberians go to the polls for the second time in a month and only the third time in a decade. Even from Washington, I can sense the momentum moving our way, but I am afraid to let myself think beyond the moment. The three days of waiting for the results are unbearable, and I am perpetually on edge. I feel so inadequate trying to gain advanced information by tapping and refreshing my Google search for Liberia + election. I scroll through the Liberian-based online media, but that only adds to the torture. Liberian media is riddled with paid-for lies and rumor.

On Friday, November 11, just before dawn, the muffled ring of my cell phone, rumbles under my pillow.

"Hold for the President-elect," says a voice I do not recognize.

"Riva, we did it!" It is Ellen. And then she is gone.

The call is over.

Adrenaline rushes through me. The news is beyond belief. Echoing in my head is that wonderful pronoun, *we*.

I jump out of bed and rush to my computer to see the news for myself, my cell phone still attached to my ear, unable to decide what to do next as I take in the enormity of this moment. It is one of elation, of pure joy, a feeling of triumph that anyone who has ever worked on a winning campaign never forgets.

With 91 percent of the votes in, Liberia's National Electoral Commission declares Ellen Johnson Sirleaf the president of the Republic of Liberia with 59.4 percent of the vote to Weah's 40.6 percent.

The voters are decisive.

I stare out the window at all of the fall foliage I have yet to rake and reflect on all that Ellen has overcome to get to the office she will soon occupy—imprisonment, threats of rape and even death, exiled from her home—I want to cry from the sheer beauty and heroics of this moment. I think back to that day in Northern Virginia, pregnant and trying to hide it, pleading with Ellen for a chance to work for her, to come along on her journey that I knew even then would be historic. I think, too of Oma and how proud she would be of me and Ellen, of us all, for having the courage to fight against the long odds and not give up. It is this kind of courage that Oma has always embodied for me. Then it occurs to me that Ellen Johnson Sirleaf is my Oma now, my Oma here in the world of the living.

The next day, headlines around the world—from the *New York Times*, the *Washington Post*, the *Financial Times,* the *International Herald Tribune*, and from newspapers large and small everywhere on every continent—trumpet the glorious, historic news: "A First for Africa: Woman Wins the Presidency of Liberia."

Ellen walking red carpet on Inauguration Day, Monrovia, January 2006.

TWELVE

THE INAUGURATION

Monrovia, Liberia
January, 2006

January 16, 2006, Monrovia. It is a hot day for Ellen's inauguration: 95 degrees with 98 percent humidity. After 20 years of travel to some of the hottest countries on the planet, my body should have acclimated to the heat and my stomach to the local cuisine by now. Not even close. Without my Cipro, yet another local doctor would be affixing an IV bag to the floor lamp in my hotel room and pumping me with fluids. But on this magical day, I put those concerns aside. Today we make history.

Ellen Johnson Sirleaf, 67, is the first democratically elected woman to lead an African nation. This mother of four has survived many storms. She has tried twice before to become Liberia's leader, but both times, in 1997 and 2003, warlord Charles Taylor robbed her of victory, and both times the US and most of the international community looked the other way.

But she who laughs last, laughs best.

As Ellen waits to take her place on stage and be sworn in as Liberia's new president, Charles Taylor sits in exile in southern Nigeria. In a final and fitting irony, it is Ellen as the new president who will decide whether Taylor stands trial for the 11 counts of crimes against humanity handed down by the Special Court of Sierra Leone. I have no doubt what her decision will be.

Ellen has been called "the Iron Lady," but Margaret Thatcher, the original holder of the title, never faced the obstacles that Ellen has faced and overcome. Although she has received numerous accolades and international awards, no prize can be worth more to Ellen than to be chosen by her own people to lead the country. Now, after 20 years of exile, and beyond the age of retirement, she finally receives that honor.

I am back at the Urban Villa, grateful to have a room in this over-packed town, with or without running water. Every hotel room and every spare bedroom in Monrovia is occupied and every functioning vehicle commandeered. People keep showing up from all over the world, most without visas or invitations. Somehow the people of Liberia find accommodations for their new visitors. This morning at breakfast, a Ghanaian woman—a member of a delegation of African women leaders—summed it up best when she exclaimed, "I would have swum the width of the ocean to be here today!" Getting from Accra to Monrovia is hard enough.

I am assigned a barely functioning 1995 Cadillac, which we have already jump-started twice. On the morning of Ellen's inauguration, as if on cue, the jalopy stalls on the single hill in downtown Monrovia, just beyond City Hall. As the car starts rolling backwards, our driver slams on the brake. Our traveling party of Americans and Ghanaians piles out of the car. We thrust a generous tip into our driver's hand, and trot toward the inaugural parade grounds. We never see the Caddy or our driver again.

The inaugural grounds are decorated with hundreds of Liberian flags. The single white star against the background of blue, red and white stripes resonates with new meaning. Liberia is known as the Lone Star State of Africa. Today Ellen is that star. Along the red carpet, that extends the length of a football field, are rows of white plastic chairs beneath the woven, thatched covering meant to shade us from the baking sun.

Every Liberian that I encounter on this special day seems to carry a spark of light within. Perhaps it is the hope for this land that has seen so much sorrow and suffered from such neglect. Now Liberians are ready to rebuild. The destruction is over. If elation were a sound, I imagine it would be like a thousand cathedral bells ringing. That is what I hear today from the throng of Liberians here for Ellen's inauguration, the ringing of their laughter and their cheers. Many of them, dressed in their soiled T-shirts and flip-flops, their usual daily attire, crowd outside the main gate to get a glimpse of their new leader. Their faces seem to glow with pride.

As I scan the block of over 5,000 invited guests, I see a pulsing mass of extraordinary color. Many of the African women attending wear traditional dresses in every shade and hue imaginable. The scene looks like an extra-large box of Crayola crayons in human form.

Ellen's campaign workers and volunteers sit in the back rows. You can identify them by the official inaugural fabric stitched into the specially-made shirts, pants, dresses, skirts, and headscarfs. The fabric depicts Ellen's likeness within a presidential seal, against a white backdrop. The words, "Her Excellency Ellen Johnson Sirleaf, President of the Republic of Liberia," appear in red, underscored in blue.

It is 10:30 a.m. The ceremony starts in thirty minutes and I don't see Amara anywhere. It's just like Amara to be late again, I grumble to myself. I have to fend off takers of the single empty seat beside me and they are getting more insistent. Finally, I spot the shiny perspiring head of the otherwise immaculate Amara in his smart, dark-blue suit. He is stuck behind the rope barrier because he forgot his VIP ticket. "That seat is for him," I plead with the Liberian National Police officer assigned to crowd control. "He is a special guest of the president! He has come all the way from America!" The officer hesitates a moment, looking stern, but then smiles and allows Amara through. The new Liberia, I think, will be different. A kinder place. "Okay, the inauguration can start now," I say to Amara and give him a hug. He is one of this nation's new heroes.

Behind the stage rises the six-story National Assembly building, once white but now stained gray. It is peppered with bullet holes from decades of civil war. Inside, there is not a single working toilet. The building is a grim reminder of Charles Taylor. How many died under Taylor? We may never have a final count. Some have said that under him Liberia lost her soul, and now Ellen has returned to restore it. The building bears witness.

As the besuited, all-male African presidents take their seats—among them Nigeria's Olusegun Obasanjo, South Africa's Thabo Mbeki, John Kufuor from Ghana, Lansana Conté of Guinea, Laurent Gbagbo of the

Ivory Coast, and Idriss Déby of Chad—they still seem slightly shocked by Ellen's ascendance to their rank. To my mind, their expressions say, *You've got to be kidding—a woman? How the hell did she pull this off? Had I known she was going to win, I wouldn't have refused to see her before the election.* I can't help but wonder what these leaders think of our winning slogan: Ellen—, She's our Man! Now, she's Africa's woman.

Passionate applause fills the grounds and I look down the carpet to see America's First Lady Laura Bush, wearing a creamy light-green outfit, and Secretary of State Condoleezza Rice, dressed in a peach linen jacket and beige skirt. Both wear rather large, matching Breton-style hats with ample round crowns and upturned brims. The two women appear fresh and cool, not a bead of sweat in sight.

As Bush and Rice pass by in a dignified stroll, I recall the off-the-record responses I received from US government officials when I tried to rally support for Ellen's campaign.

It's a traditional society—the tribal leaders will not accept a woman.

You're wasting your time.

Weah's got the election in the bag.

I remember all the journalists I contacted in an effort to gain media attention for Ellen, the ones who didn't return my calls and the ones who told me flat-out that their publications were only interested in covering George Weah. His election to the presidency was a foregone conclusion. This morning he is still an international soccer star. Ellen Johnson Sirleaf is president.

Weah now sits in the front row of the inaugural crowd, perhaps the most shocked guest in attendance—and he looks it. For a professional athlete, sportsmanship didn't come easily. Following the internationally monitored election results, he claimed fraud and declared himself the rightful president. It sparked rioting in Monrovia. Finally, after much national and international pressure, he conceded Ellen's victory. But the world had noted the red card he had been served.

What's George thinking now? I wonder. That "old lady" is now Her Excellency, President of the Republic of Liberia. His president.

By all accounts, Ellen shouldn't be here. On many occasions she teetered dangerously close to becoming a footnote in history, and over the years, I had come to know her stories of defeat well. There was the day in 1985 when Master Sergeant Samuel Doe ordered her arrest. When two soldiers came for her, Ellen engaged them in conversation, throwing them off-balance. Her cleverness was her best weapon. The two began to argue about whether they were supposed to take her to a field and kill her or bring her to jail. Confused and unsure, she nudged them to choose the second option and her life was spared.

Shortly after Ellen's imprisonment, a naked woman, abused and raped by the prison guards, was tossed into Ellen's cell. Clearly, Ellen was slated for the same treatment. But one guard looked at her and, referring to one of Liberia's 16 ethnic groups, said, "Some say you are Gola," the prominent tribe from the northwest, and one of the oldest.

"It is true," she answered.

"Say something in the Gola language," he demanded.

Ellen complied. After hearing her words, the guard, a Grebo from Maryland County who spoke the same dialect, offered to sleep in her cell so that she would not be attacked and raped. This former guard later became Ellen's aide-de-camp.

Suddenly, all heads turn as the announcer declares that the inaugural procession is about to begin. Ellen leads the procession. She wears a broad smile as she pivots and waves to the crowd and to the world. Africa's first woman president is being celebrated globally. The international media has come for the event, including NBC's Today Show host Ann Curry, people from CNN, and so many more. Ellen is ready for this moment. Striding down the carpet, she looks like an African queen, a democratically elected one, dressed in a white and gold gown with a traditional headscarf fastened together with a series of gold pins. It looks like a crown.

Her eyes shine through her small gold-rimmed glasses. In a campaign where being "authentically" African is measured by skin tone, Ellen's lighter shade, a product of her German trader grandfather, was a liability. Ellen repeatedly had to remind her electorate she is not an Americo-Liberian, the small five percent minority whose mismanagement of the country's resources continues to cause riffs in the debate over national identity. "I am indigenous," she said, over and over again.

Ellen is even wearing makeup this morning, an unusual occurrence. It is a far cry from the blue jeans, baseball cap, and muck boots she donned on the campaign trail. She is also twenty pounds lighter and looking fit and energetic from trudging tirelessly around the country. Despite the fact that armed Taylor loyalists are everywhere and her life is still in danger, Ellen does not betray the slightest hint of fear.

A month earlier on a trip I arranged for her to Washington, DC, as president-elect, Ellen met with Secretary of Defense Donald Rumsfeld, Secretary of State Condoleezza Rice, and selected members of Congress. I made sure to push the issue of Ellen's safety, including at the inauguration. As a result, $20 million was re-programmed and directed toward security for her. I breathe a sigh of relief now, seeing her flanked by US Secret Service agents with their trademark cropped hair, dark suits, coiled earpieces, and Ray-Ban sunglasses. Even more impressive, on view from the inaugural grounds, are two US Naval ships, the USS *Carr* and the USS *Mount Whitney*, anchored just offshore as powerful symbols of US support for the Sirleaf presidency.

Walking at Ellen's side now is her 72-year-old sister, Jennie. Our eyes meet and she shakes her head and smiles, as if to say, "I can't believe she really did it." I smile back. Almost ten years earlier I became a de facto member of Ellen's family. I remember Jennie's first call when she urged me to persuade Ellen not to run against Taylor. "We fear for her life," She had said. We both knew then that neither of us could convince Ellen not to run.

In the first row, I see Ellen's sons assembled, James, Charles, Rob, and Adamah, and behind them, their spouses and a cluster of grandchildren. I think about the way ambitious women have to piece it all together. Ellen had given birth to her sons in quick succession, starting when she was 19. Mother and children practically grew up together, but because of the circumstances of her life, they often had to endure being apart. Last night, her family hovered around her. I felt like one of them myself as I moved around the living room and then showed her different drafts of the inaugural speech. Ellen sat in a corner chair, across from a 2,000-piece jigsaw puzzle that she constantly fiddled with. They were just a regular family, like any other, and they paid no attention to the fact that their mother and grandmother was famous. Ellen made it a point to not fuss. I had never met James, Charles or Rob before, but Adamah I knew. Adamah is a doctor in northwest Connecticut, and when he was not on-call or in the ER during these past months, he was working on his mom's campaign, energizing the Liberian diaspora.

I did not know what Ellen was thinking with all the commotion around us. No one ever really does. But I imagine her saying to herself, *My dear family—thank you for all of your sacrifices. I pray you believe that it was worth it.*

As Ellen reaches the stage now, my eyes sweep the members of the legislature seated behind her red and gold, throne-like chair. Prominent among them is Speaker of the House, Edwin Snowe, accused of stealing millions of dollars from a Liberian oil company; Senator Adolphus Dolo, known during the war as "General Peanut Butter" after his favorite food and accused of eating his victims' body parts; Senator Prince Johnson, the former rebel leader who hacked off President Samuel Doe's ears before killing him in 1990; and finally, to the surprise of many outsiders, Senator Jewel Howard Taylor, the former First Lady to ex-president Charles Taylor. All of them are among the many powerful Liberian politicians who did not want Ellen to succeed, and still don't. They are here now, basking in the glory that their former nemesis has bestowed on this nation.

Ellen takes her seat on the grand chair as Edwin Snowe, the new Speaker of the House, is sworn in. He then takes a seat behind Ellen and proceeds to place a large top hat on his head. For those in the know, it is a power-play message to her that he will not be subservient to her leadership. I watch as she registers the moment, but doesn't react. She begins her inaugural address, which I pretty much know by heart.

Ellen pauses, looks intently at the crowd, then veers from her prepared message and turns directly to Mr. Snowe, addressing him—and his hat.

"Everyone will be required to declare his assets. I will be the first to comply, and I will call upon the Honorable Speaker and President Pro-Tem to say that they will comply."

The audience erupts with applause and shouts and cheers of "Amen!"

"We pledge anew," Ellen continues, "our commitment to transparency, open government, and participatory democracy for all of our citizens."

"Amen to that," I whisper.

I have spent nearly two decades working with countries in transition from war to peace, from dictatorship to democracy. Whatever the role, my goals have remained fundamentally the same: to impact public policy in a positive way, to shape public opinion, and when lucky, to support a people striving for democracy. Sometimes in a very small way, and sometimes in a not-so-small way, I have been an active participant in shaping the course of events, both at home and overseas. More often than not, I have believed fully in what I was doing, and in the people and the causes I supported. On occasion, though, I have been assigned duties where the morality of a situation is far from certain, the ambitions of certain players less than noble. In those cases, I can only do my best to limit the damage while I try not to focus on the self-accusatory question, *Why am I here?* And sometimes, much more rarely, I find myself working alongside someone like Ellen. That is when it all comes together, the pride, the joy, the satisfaction in knowing that in fact, yes, we just might leave this world a better place than we found it.

Today, at this moment of triumph here in Monrovia, I am in a reflective mood. Mine has been a career of adventure and drudgery, of public speeches and backroom politicking, a world of redeemers and killers, true believers and corrupt cynics, hope and despair, and in instances such as Ellen's inauguration, of celebration and euphoria. Throughout my career I have often wondered just how much difference individual acts can make when the Big Picture is out of your control, or when your government and its proxies decide to change sides and you decide not to follow. History can be made in different ways—not only by the generals or the elected (and unelected) officials, but sometimes by the efforts of anonymous people who work, plan, scheme, manipulate, even horse-trade behind the scenes in order to achieve our goals. I have learned to appreciate the truly awesome power of the United States Government, and I have come to know its limitations. I am reminded today that people around the world continue to fight and die for the principles that our country was founded upon, principles that most Americans take for granted. Democracy with all its nuances and imprecision is exported every day, often self-servingly, through individual and collective acts of truth and defiance. It is our country's greatest and most ambitious gift to the world. But there is also the brutal truth that in mission after mission, country after country, people don't always have the option to live to fight another day. Power is complex and utterly unpredictable, a gift and a curse. Some of the candidates I supported did not win. Others have won and have failed at fulfilling their promise. Some of the opposition leaders I have worked with were subsequently killed. That is the nature of high-stakes international politics, and one of the reasons for the question that frequently visits me: *Why am I here?* I have asked myself countless times, wondering how much of my work assisting world leaders has also contributed to their demise. Have we pushed too hard and too early for ideals that cannot work? Have we opened political debate only to ignite decades-old tribal conflicts? Have we moved too quickly? Have we ignored historical and cultural realities? Did we support the right side? I wish I had a simple answer to the questions. But power and democracy can be both complex and unpredictable.

The crowd erupts in cheers and jolts me from my reverie. I rise and join in the applause as Ellen continues.

"I make this pledge to you. We will work to ensure that papa and mama will come home joyfully with something, no matter how meager, to sustain their family. We will make the children smile again!"

There is my answer. I know why I am here.

Washington Post, day after Ellen addresses Joint Session of Congress, March 16, 2006.

THIRTEEN

ADDRESSING THE US CONGRESS

Washington, DC
March 2006

After a great deal of behind-the-scenes maneuvering, we are ready to announce the news to the United States and the rest of the world. On March 15, 2006, at 2:00 p.m. EST, the president of the Republic of Liberia will address a joint meeting of the US Congress. Ellen will become only the fourth African leader to be given the honor. The last time an African ascended the podium before Congress was in 1994; the speaker was Nelson Mandela.

My firm has consented to allow me to register with the United States Department of Justice, required under US law, so I can officially represent the government of Liberia. I am no longer working for an individual. I am working for a foreign state and thus need to be registered and recognized as such. It is the law. Further, to my pleasant surprise, they agree to let me do the work pro bono—until such time as resources can be mobilized. Even BKSH management now appreciates the PR value of associating with Ellen Johnson Sirleaf.

The invitation to address Congress is negotiated with a strong push from Minority Leader Nancy Pelosi, who will soon make her own history and become the first female Speaker of the House of Representatives. Pelosi's staff petitioned the office of Speaker Dennis Hastert every day, without mercy. Backing Pelosi were leaders from Hastert's own party: Congressman Ed Royce (R-CA), Chairman of the Africa Subcommittee of House Foreign Affairs, Senate Majority Leader Bill Frist (R-TN) and Senator Richard Lugar (R-IN), Chairman of the Senate Foreign Relations Committee. But even without the lobbying, and despite the shrinking bipartisan consensus on foreign policy in the Congress, this one was a pretty easy call for Hastert.

President Sirleaf will be honored later in the week with a luncheon at the White House hosted by President Bush and First Lady Laura Bush, part of the program organized by the Assistant Secretary of State for African Affairs, Jendayi Frazer. But this visit, Ellen's first to DC as the President of the Republic of Liberia, as the first elected woman head of state on the African continent, is primarily dedicated to her appearance before the US Congress.

Ellen understands well that US Administrations come and go. How many had she seen? Jimmy Carter, Ronald Reagan, George H.W. Bush, Bill Clinton, George W. Bush. But it is the US Congress, and through them, the American people, that she will always need to rely on and speak to directly.

We arrange for Ellen to use a holding room near the Capitol Rotunda, courtesy of the House Sergeant of Arms, as her base of operations for two days. She goes from here to her dizzying schedule of door-to-door meetings with the House and Senate leadership, the authorizing bodies for foreign affairs, the appropriators of foreign operations, the Congressional Black Caucus, the Congressional Women's Caucus, the delegations from states with large Liberian diasporas such as Rhode Island, and those individual members who personally supported Liberia's struggle and Ellen's struggle over the years. Ellen also has her list of influential Congressional staff, the members they work for, and others to thank in each meeting. On that personal list are two prominent politicians: Senator Hillary Rodham Clinton of New York and Senator Barack Obama of Illinois.

Her visit to Congress is not just to say thank you. Ellen is not that sentimental. Congress has the power of the purse. "I am not just coming to give a speech. I need to commercialize that good will," she admits to me.

No resting on my laurels. I know better after all this time.

With the support of Congressman Jessie Jackson Jr. and Congresswoman Nita Lowey, along with the Congressional Black Caucus, we tee up an amendment to the Emergency Supplemental Spending Bill for

Fiscal 2006 that includes a $50 million "democracy dividend" for Liberia. If things go as planned, the amendment will pass the House floor two days after Ellen gives her speech. Senate appropriators tell us that if the amendment makes it off the House floor it will be accepted by the Senate and likely packaged with a lesser amount for Haiti's newly-elected president, René Préval.

As Ellen waits in H-210 of the US Capitol, dozens of members of Congress jockey to get their picture taken with her, or better, to be the ones in the CNN and C-SPAN footage walking with Ellen as she enters the hall and ascends to the podium. Those who make it into the picture include Representative Nancy Pelosi (D-CA), Representative Donald Payne (D-NJ), Representative Elijah Cummings (D-MD), Representative John Lewis (D-GA), Senator Bill Frist (R-TN) and Senator Ted Stevens (R-Alaska).

I was up all that previous night finalizing the speech. I sent it to Rachel Perry in the Speaker's office at 10:05 a.m. that morning. Ellen didn't want me to send it.

"What if I modify it in delivery?" she asked. "I always modify my speeches."

I explained that it wouldn't matter. Congressional protocol for the joint session demands that advance copies be given to the leadership.

At precisely 2:00 p.m., Ellen enters the chamber to thunderous applause. She shakes hands, receives awkward embraces (Ellen isn't one for hugs), and receives loud shout-outs that almost feel inappropriate in that august hall. There isn't an empty seat to be found in the chamber. This time eager staffers looking for tickets come away empty-handed. Their bosses—members from both houses of Congress and from both sides of the aisle—have uncharacteristically decided to attend the ceremony themselves. Ellen seems to be doing what no one else in Washington is able to accomplish: create a bipartisan consensus. And she is smiling, which doesn't happen all that often.

"The President of the Republic of Liberia, Ellen Johnson Sirleaf" announces Speaker Hastert to an explosion of applause. Seated just off the floor in a special section designated for Ellen's guests, I am covered in goosebumps.

The applause continues unabated. Ellen, in a gesture I have seen often, presses her hands together, just under her chin, prayer-like, bows her head and tries to will silence into the hall. She looks exquisite, dressed in a black, African traditional dress, covered with embroidered red, black and gold circles, a swath of cloth across her shoulder, and a matching head scarf fastened in front with a pin in the shape of a flower.

Her audience loves her this day. Some of the most powerful and influential people on the planet stand and cheer for her, including the President of the Senate and Vice President of the United States, Dick Cheney, who is seated directly behind her.

The speech that we have timed for 27 minutes at Ellen's pace goes on for nearly forty, interrupted repeatedly by applause.

I stand before you today as the first woman elected to lead an African nation, thanks to the grace of Almighty God; thanks to the courage of the Liberian people, who chose their future over fear; thanks to the people of West Africa and of Africa generally, who continued to give hope to my people. Thanks also to President Bush whose strong resolve and public condemnation and appropriate action forced a tyrant into exile; and thanks to you—the members of this august body—who spurred the international effort that brought blessed peace to our nation.

It was the leadership of the 108th Congress, more than two years ago that paved the way for a United Nations force that secured our peace and guaranteed free and fair elections. It was your $445 million addition to a supplemental appropriations bill that attracted additional commitments from international donors. With those funds, we have laid the foundation for a durable peace, not only in Liberia, but in the whole West African sub-region.

Honorable ladies and gentlemen of this Congress, I want to thank you— all the Liberian people sent me here to thank you—for that vision. Our triumph over evil is also your triumph.

After that passage, wild applause lasts almost a full minute. Ellen goes on to give what many members in the audience later declare was one of the best speeches ever delivered before a joint meeting of Congress. Ellen concludes with this:

With your prayers and with your help, we will demonstrate that democracy can work, even under the most challenging conditions. We will honor the suffering of our people, and Liberia will become a brilliant beacon, an example to Africa and to the world of what the love of liberty can achieve. We will strive to be America's success story in Africa, demonstrating the potential in the transformation from war to peace.

On March 17 Liberia's "democracy dividend" amendment is offered on the House floor, without objection, to the Administration's supplemental spending request for Fiscal 2006. It eventually passes the Senate and is signed into law by President Bush.

♦

There is one more memorable event that year—memorable at least to me. It is nothing as momentous or internationally significant as all that Ellen has accomplished, but still, it would not have occurred without her. I finally find the courage to leave my old firm, BKSH, and start again, on my own this time.

For the past ten years I managed the international portfolio for BKSH. I had done the same for ten years prior to that at Black, Manafort, Stone & Kelly. I journeyed around the world on many adventures, sometimes thrust onto the front lines of history. No matter what trouble I got in, I could always rely on my company to be there to bail me out. There was also the security of the steady paycheck, the insurance coverage, the comfort of knowing that my bills would always be paid on time. But there was also the down side of my durability at BKSH. I was never offered partner. I did not have control of my clients or the projects that I worked on. I was always looking over my shoulder, wondering if it was my turn to be judged redundant. I never really knew if my clients valued me and my work, or whether it was my marquee partners who attracted my clients to the firm.

And there were the deeper questions. Where was I going? Could I reach my potential if I stayed within the BKSH structure? I already knew the answers. I just had to have the guts to deal with them.

I felt like one of those decorative indoor trees planted in their woven baskets, placed in the corner of an office by the window where it would grow too tall for the space, pressing at the ceiling tiles, denied the possibility to climb higher. And then there was Ellen. After all those years, all my missions, I had finally achieved something meaningful. It was a pretty amazing feeling to know that your contribution mattered and that you acted for all the right reasons. Of course I knew I couldn't sustain that sense of professional satisfaction every day. But I also knew I couldn't go back to the potpourri of empty client assignments. Whom I associated with mattered now. I work for Ellen Johnson Sirleaf, the first woman president on the African continent. I need to maintain a certain integrity in my assignments.

◆

Monday, December 11, 2006, is our first day at the new location of BKSH & Associates on Vermont Avenue. We were on K Street for more than ten years. Before the move, all employees are told to throw away everything that they don't need. "If it's not for an active client, if there is no legal requirement to keep it, or if there is no historical value for its use, toss it."

I refuse to throw anything away. Everything has historical value for me. I pack up all of my files, from Iraq to Angola, South Africa to Kashmir, Kenya to Sri Lanka, Nigeria, the Philippines, Liberia. In my new office that morning, I have 18 florescent orange plastic packing crates taking up the limited floor space of my office. I sit at my desk, hidden behind the containers. By 4:30 p.m. that day I have not unpacked a single crate. If I am going to leave, it will be now. Ellen has been elected. She will be my first client. She values me, not my company. Then, I think with a half-smile: I am already packed.

I call my husband Jeff. He is fully supportive. "You should have left years ago, Riva. Kylie and Andrew need their mom happy. You'll do great on your own. You just need to have as much confidence in yourself as everyone else does."

I put down the receiver, stare at the stack of unpacked neon crates, and let my mind drift back several decades, to one month before my graduation from Tufts University, when I drove my '75 Olds to Manhattan to see Oma. I had what I thought was an important decision to make, one I was certain would define my future. Do I take that great summer job waitressing at an exclusive restaurant on Nantucket? I'd get lots of tips, free room and board, and according to the bartender at Legal Seafood who offered me the job, I would have "the time of my life." At twenty-something, we all know what that means. But I also had the option of moving to Washington, DC, for an unpaid summer internship with the Los Angeles Olympic Organizing Committee (LAOOC). I could teach aerobics during my lunch hour and rent a spare bedroom from a friend of a friend. The internship would be good for my career and my resume. But it is hard to refuse "the time of your life." I needed Oma's wisdom; we always need someone to help us see the bigger picture.

Oma had gotten all dressed up for my visit, wearing a beige and brown woolen dress, with a scarf tied around her shoulders and her heavy beige support stockings. "So unnecessary," I told Oma. "If not for you, than for who? Even at my age," she answered. "It is important to keep up one's appearances." We sat down to a bowl of her baked oatmeal mixed with cottage cheese, apple sauce and canned sweet peaches, which she knew I loved. She handed me a heavy silver spoon. "So?" she asked. I explained to her the decision that burdened me. She listened intently and quietly let me finish. She smiled and understood. "Can I tell you a story?"

"Okay," I replied, though impatient for her advice.

"When I was a young child, eight years old, the same age your mother was when we left for America, I had almost been killed, right in my own bedroom, in our home. I was in my bed, the lantern was off, and my mother had just said good night. It was quiet and dark, and all of the sudden the ceiling burst open above me, wood and debris rained down, and the entire house shook. I buried myself under the covers and waited, fearful and confused for what seemed like a long time. Then my mother and father, my sisters and our caretaker ran into my bedroom. At first I thought I had done something wrong and I would be blamed. And there—," my grandmother pointed at the coffee table, "about a meter from my bed, was a bomb—a gigantic, gray, cast in metal bomb with a tail. It had fallen through the ceiling but had not exploded. My mother clutched me too hard and I felt her fear. We didn't know if it was Russian or German, only that it hadn't exploded. My father swept me out of my bed and we all rushed outside for the rest of the night. My parents said this was a sign of what was coming in Europe, and we abandoned our house. We grabbed our most cherished belongings that we could carry, and headed to the countryside."

Oma slowed her speech and cast her eyes downward. I was so engrossed in my grandmother's story I nearly forgot my summer dilemma.

"Why didn't you tell me this story before?" I asked. "Are you saying that I need to enjoy the moment now because we don't know what will happen tomorrow?"

"It is your decision to make, dear Riva. There is so much that we don't control in this world and you can never be certain which decisions will have consequence. Sometimes, what seems to be the most trivial can define a life. Sometimes it's the opposite. If that the bomb had fallen a meter to the left or had exploded, neither of us would be here today to decide anything." She smiled and I understood.

At 5:35 p.m. I go down the hall to visit with my bosses, Charlie Black and Scott Pastrick. And I quit.

That weekend, Kylie, Andrew, Jeff and I have a moving party. Three months later, on March 15, 2007, I open KRL International LLC. It is scary, jumping into the void, suddenly being your own boss, taking responsibility for the success or failure of a company. But I draw on valuable lessons in courage from the woman I admire, and I gain strength from her. I am confident that things will work out.

THE DARKEST CHALLENGE YET: EBOLA

Washington, DC
Summer, 2014

It is Monday, July 28, 2014, one week before the convening of the first African Leaders' Summit by President Barack Obama. The White House extends invitations to all African leaders in good standing with the US—49 of the 54 nations on the continent. All 49 countries have announced their intention to send a delegation, and 37 heads of state have confirmed their attendance. Thirty-seven African leaders in the US capital at once, an immense feat. Only Robert Mugabe of Zimbabwe, Omar al-Bashir of the Sudan, interim president Catherine Samba-Panza of Central African Republic, Isaias Afewerki of Eritrea, and Mohamed Abdelaziz of the Sahrawi Arab Democratic Republic are excluded from the list.

A full program of meetings is organized for Ellen on the margins of the summit, where all the real business gets done. But now I have doubts that she will come at all. There is something far more pressing that demands her attention at home.

For nearly a year, the deadly Ebola virus disease, one of the most feared contagions in the world, has been spreading slowly in southern Guinea, which shares 350 miles of its porous southern border with Liberia, from Mendekoma to Nimba. The world gradually begins to learn the fearsome details of the virus: a single microscopic trace of a bodily fluid from an infected person or corpse can quickly destroy a healthy body, resulting in an agonizing death in which the victim bleeds uncontrollably, internally and externally.

Until now, the outbreak has attracted scant notice of the global health community. The first human host is thought to be a 2-year-old boy who may have contracted the disease from the feces of an infected fruit bat. From that single touch, the child, members of the child's immediate family, his extended family, his community, and his caregivers become infected. The child dies. Many of the others will die within weeks of his burial.

And then, it is theorized, the disease hops a ride on a motorbike carrying a young Liberian woman who attends a family wedding just across the border where the states of Guinea, Liberia and Sierra Leone are indistinguishable from one another. The young woman falls ill some days later and goes to Redemption Hospital on Bushrod Island, across the bridge from downtown Monrovia. She is attended to by a number of nurses and one of the hospital's few medical doctors. The initial diagnosis is malaria. She will die days later and eventually so will everyone at Redemption who provided her care.

The motorbike driver, a young man who made a living ferrying Liberians to their families across the border, returns to his home in Monrovia, the West Point area, after dropping off his passenger. It was a good day's work and he is tired. Eight days later he too will be sick. He never makes it to a hospital but dies in agony in his house, which like most dwellings in West Point, has no running water or electricity. He infects several of his friends and members of his family.

From that motorbike transport and other seemingly random movements of people crossing the border from Guinea, Ebola will begin to spread uncontrollably in Liberia and in neighboring Sierra Leone. *Medecins Sans Frontières (MSF)* has been warning for months that the disease in Guinea has not burned out as hoped, but that the few cases that have emerged in Liberia and Sierra Leone are the harbinger of a major chain of transmission that needs to be understood and managed aggressively with more resources and personnel than are currently available. The World Health Organization (WHO), paralyzed by its own bureaucracy and the enormity of the problem, does not respond to MSF's pleas.

The government of Liberia is likewise slow to recognize the danger that the country is facing. Both the Minister of Health and the Minister of Information deny a healthcare crisis exists. There is no experience with the disease outside of the Democratic Republic of Congo and Uganda. In those cases, the outbreak occurred in remote and isolated locations. For the first time, here in West Africa, the outbreak has gone urban.

Now it hits, seemingly all at once, in Liberia.

Healthcare workers begin dying. Hospitals and clinics close their doors. The sick begin hiding from their families, willing to die alone in the streets to avoid infecting their loved ones. Fear overwhelms. One eight-year-old girl, left alone in her rural village home in Lofa country, lies beside her dead mother, crying in pain and screaming for help, while her neighbors stay away for fear of infecting themselves—until the cries stop and the girl is dead.

There are so many stories of pain and loss, and about the shame of those who are too afraid to help others. Such non-response is alien to this community-based culture where everyone in a village is considered part of an extended family.

By July 30, 156 deaths are confirmed in Liberia, with the number of sick rising almost exponentially every day. The predictions are dire. If the disease continues on its current trajectory, tens of thousands will be infected by October. No one knows after that.

President Sirleaf makes the decision to shut down all schools and force a mandatory 30-day leave for all government officials. In neighboring Sierra Leone, a state of emergency is declared. President Sirleaf is contemplating the same in Liberia. The president orders the quarantining of sick communities—no one is to go in or out unless they are security or healthcare workers. The Armed Forces of Liberia monitor the quarantine. There is fear and a sense of abandonment in the affected populations. The quarantines are a mistake. The Liberian government will soon figure out the best way to contain the virus: community policing.

By the end of July, Ebola has also spread by air. Patrick Sawyer, a healthcare consultant whose pregnant sister has just died of a hemorrhage in her third trimester, boards a flight from Monrovia to Lagos,

Nigeria, where he plans to take a connecting flight to the United States. He collapses in the Lagos airport and is taken to a local hospital, delirious and near death. He dies soon after. Fifty-nine contacts are identified, including 13 healthcare workers who came in touch with his bodily fluids. Several will die.

President Sirleaf is in touch 24/7 with MSF and other not-for-profits operating the few Ebola Treatment Units (ETUs) in the country. She is trying to understand the clinical scope of the crisis so she can advocate for the most effective international response. We need resources, MSF tells her, dozens more ETUs, including in remote locations, personal protective equipment, hydration kits, antibiotics, laboratory capacity, vehicles, and most important, additional personnel. MSF is out of funds and volunteers. They are calling for a military-style mobilization, with special units that have biohazard capability. "That's what it will take," MSF personnel tells President Sirleaf.

But what do you do while waiting for help to arrive? How do you cope while having to rely on a post-conflict healthcare system that can barely treat the sick in the best of times, in a country that has only 218 doctors and 5,200 nurses to care for a population of 4.3 million across 15 counties, most of them remote without paved roads, electricity or potable water?

◆

It is 2:45 p.m. and I am in the security line at the Voice of America building on Independence Avenue in Washington, getting ready to escort a client, a prominent African business leader, into the building. He will do an interview to help set the stage for Obama's African Leaders Summit. I have prepared him with sample questions.

What would this historic gathering, the first in the history of the Oval Office, mean for the changing dynamic between the US and Africa? Is there a real shift towards a private-sector approach where trade and investment trump foreign assistance? Will the United States ever catch up to China on the African continent?

We are already late. My phone vibrates: an incoming call with the 231 country-code. I answer immediately.

"Hold the line for Madam President," orders Phemie Brewer, Ellen's executive assistant.

"I have to take this call," I announce to my client, "It's an emergency."

Ellen comes on the line. "Riva, I will not attend the Summit," she announces. "I am sending the vice president in my place."

"I was expecting this call," I reply, knowing full well the reason she has to stay in Liberia.

"I called Ambassador Malac," says Ellen, referring to Liberia's US Ambassador. "She is already in the States for the Summit. She tells me that the White House is not pleased."

"Don't worry about that," I advise, but I am outraged that Ellen has to deal with an expression of diplomatic dissatisfaction in Washington while at home she is facing a life-and-death crisis.

"The Ebola outbreak is one of the hardest things that I have ever faced in my life," says Ellen. "I have never felt so helpless."

I move to a shaded area outside the VOA building. Tears well in my eyes. Ellen sounds scared. And that absolutely terrifies me.

◆

It has been a remarkable ride, those eight years following Ellen's address to the Joint Meeting of Congress in March 2006. It felt then that nothing could halt her momentum, at home or abroad. There was the announcement of Liberia's first 150-day Plan, the implementation of Liberia's post-conflict development strategy, the government's success in reaching the Heavily Indebted Poor Countries (HIPC) Completion Point with the International Monetary Fund (IMF) and the World Bank, and of course the unprecedented deal for the repayment of Liberia's commercial debt at three cents on the dollar, negotiated under the leadership of Liberia's Finance Minister Antoinette Sayeh with the counsel of Steven Radelet, a former US Treasury official. That was a post-conflict first, and it set the stage for economic growth.

Ellen returned to Congress each year and successfully appealed for riders to emergency funding bills to support Liberia's security sector reform, including the reconstitution of the Armed Forces of Liberia and the establishment of an Emergency Response Unit (ERU). "Other than the Israeli Prime Minister, no foreign leader works the Hill like Ellen," remarked her supporters at the ONE Campaign, the non-profit organization founded by Bono to fight extreme poverty.

There were the whirlwind international tours where Ellen accepted awards and honors, one after another, including the 2007 President Medal of Freedom from George W. Bush, and 14 honorary degrees from American colleges and universities. *Newsweek* magazine listed her as one of the ten best leaders in the world. She made the *TIME* 100, and *The Economist* called her "the best President the country has ever had.

Then came the crowning moment when Ellen accepted the most prestigious prize of them all, the 2011 Nobel Peace Prize, which she shared with fellow Liberian activist Leymah Gbowee and Yemeni women's rights advocate Tawakkol Karman. The *Financial Times* published a Special Report on Liberia and distributed it at the ceremony in Oslo with a commemorative wrapper and poster of President Sirleaf.

Momentum in politics, however, never lasts.

The same year Ellen won the Nobel she ran for a second term, even though, like Nelson Mandela, she had declared earlier that she would serve only one term. Going back on that promise was not easy, and not without political backlash. But she deemed it essential. "I need to ensure that our path is irreversible," said Ellen.

It turned out to be a bruising campaign. In a *Newsweek* cover story, "Fighting for Survival," the same Prue Clarke who had hailed Ellen's rise six years earlier at the Unity Party Convention, who could even be credited with predicting it, now reported that Ellen was "acclaimed overseas and unpopular at home" and that "she most certainly could lose the presidential contest." *Newsweek* was not alone. Most other international news outlets said the same. That assumption was being fed to the media by Ellen's main opposition, the Congress for Democratic Change (CDC), this time with aging soccer star George Weah second on the ticket to

Winston Tubman, a legacy Liberian politician. Ellen's imminent defeat became doctrine for the CDC cadre.

Ellen won the first round of the election with 44 percent, shy of the 50 percent needed to avoid a run-off election, which was not unexpected in a field of 16 candidates. She was prepared for a second round. The CDC was not, again. Winning just 32 percent of the vote, they cried foul, charging that the election had been rigged. Whether they really believed they had been wronged, or whether it was a just a crass maneuver for political leverage, is debatable. Nonetheless, they backed themselves into a corner. As the second round of voting neared, and the political tide turned against them, the CDC called for a boycott of the elections and took to the streets.

On Monday, November 7, 2011, one day before the scheduled second round, the Emergency Response Police (ERU), the only police force allowed under Liberian law to carry weapons, were mobilized and positioned across the street from CDC headquarters to prevent the protesters from blocking Tubman Boulevard, the route that carried all traffic to and from downtown Monrovia. Any disruption to Tubman would effectively shut down the capital.

"Don't overreact to provocation," the ERU forces were instructed that morning by Liberia's National Security Council. "The whole world is watching."

"Do not allow violence to mar Liberia's consolidation of its young democracy," urged the US Ambassador, Linda Thomas Greenfield, appealing to government and opposition supporters alike.

I was on Tubman Boulevard two kilometers from Ellen's house when the traffic came to a dead stop. I received a call from the Minister of Defense, Brownie Samukai. "Shots have been fired at the CDC headquarters. If you're en route, go back towards Mamba Point."

Suddenly, everyone around me was on cell phones. The CDC was claiming that there were dozens dead, although no one yet could confirm the figure. Rumors traveled with the speed of voice and text message. No one, including me, knew what to do or what would happen next. Local businesses on the main road began to close, pulling metal shutters across their windows to protect them from rioters. My first instinct was flight and self-preservation, to move back towards town and neutral ground, then wait it out at the Royal Hotel. But my sense of mission got the best of me. This is an incident, not a cycle of renewed violence, I reasoned. How the government responds to this crisis will define Liberia's democratic future. I needed to get to Ellen."

I dialed Phemie. "Madam President is on the campaign trail in the Buchanan area," I was told. "She is now headed back to her home. You can meet her there."

With the streets jammed like a parking lot, I eventually had to get out of my vehicle and walk towards Ellen's home, fielding all kinds of calls along the way—the US ambassador, the US agency providing technical assistance to the National Electoral Commission, and my son, Andrew.

"CNN is reporting that violence is breaking out across Liberia," Andrew announced before I could ask him how he was doing.

"It was a single incident. Conflict sells. You know that." I answered him with a conviction I did not really feel. "I am fine," I told Andrew. "Let Dad know."

As it turned out, there was no cycle of violence beginning in Monrovia that day, although two deaths were confirmed. The details were still murky, but the intent was to muddy the otherwise peaceful political process. The killings were a shock, the first politically-related deaths in nearly a decade. The incident was a blow to the national psyche.

Two days later, the morning following the vote, I sat with Ellen, her sister Jennie and other supporters in the "Palava Hut," adjacent to her home, listening to reports on the local radio stations. Ellen was winning with 90 percent of the vote. But because of the boycott and the violence, the turnout, which had been nearly 80 percent during the first round, was now barely 30 percent.

It was a typical Liberian morning during the dry season, very hot and humid, but the intermittent fans provided some relief as we sat together on the wicker furniture that adorns the presidential sitting room. We tried to decide what emotion it was fair to own that day. Those around Ellen were celebrating her victory each time a radio report confirmed another polling station or regional tally for Ellen. Ellen was listening intently, continuously adjusting the radio antenna and swatting away mosquitoes. She was smiling at the reactions of her friends and family. But there was no smile in her eyes. She then turned to me and said, "I feel robbed of the sweetness of this election victory." She paused, and continued with her thoughts, "The political immaturity in the country could well represent one of our greatest challenges going forward."

That second presidential campaign, the election violence and its aftermath, represented my lowest moment working with Ellen as the president of the Republic of Liberia. That is, until Ebola hit.

♦

"We need help." The urgency in Ellen's voice is clear through the static of the transatlantic call. "MSF says we need a full-scale mobilization by donor countries that are equipped with special biohazard capability. But we don't even have enough latex gloves for our own medical personnel! We need the US military," she concludes.

I catch myself before Ellen can get any hint of how frightened I feel for her and everyone around her. A thought crosses my mind and freezes me. What if Ellen becomes sick? But at that moment I need to be professional and start figuring out a way to help.

"We won't have any success raising the alarm with the administration today," I tell her. "They have 37 African heads-of-state arr*iving in town."

"Then you need to speak with your friends in Congress," Ellen counters.

"They are recessing on Friday," I reply, but add quickly, "There's a chance that we can get some key people on calls in the next couple of days."

"They will respond to Liberia's plea," Ellen declares, "as they always have. They must begin to raise their voices for an aggressive US mobilization."

I know what Ellen does not need to say. Every hour we delay means more victims of the disease. I turn for coordinating help to Christopher Beatty, my colleague of seven years, an intense and passionate 28-year-old who carries himself like a US Secret Service Agent, tall, slim, erect posture, serious expression, always aware of his surroundings—which is useful, given our international assignments.

In 48 hours Chris manages to schedule calls with half of the US Congressional leadership, nabbing the personal cell phone numbers of senators, breaking through layers of blocking and tackling by front-office staff. He even locates a couple of members on vacation. In two days Ellen speaks with Minority Leader Nancy Pelosi, Representative Ed Royce (R-CA), now the Chairman of the House Foreign Affairs Committee, Representative Chris Smith (R-NJ), Chairman of the House Subcommittee for Africa, Human Rights and Global Health, Representative Karen Bass (D-CA), Ranking member of the same, Representative Nita Lowey (D-NJ), Ranking member of the Foreign Operations Appropriations Committee, Senator Patrick Leahy (D-VT), Chairman of the Senate Foreign Operations Appropriations Subcommittee, Senator Lindsey Graham (R-SC), Ranking Republican of the same, Senator Chris Coons (D-DE), Chairman of the Africa Subcommittee of the Senate Foreign Relations Committee, Senator Jeff Flake (R-AZ), Ranking Republican of the same, and Senator John McCain (R-AZ), Chairman of the Senate Armed Services Committee.

In every call Ellen explains the crisis that Liberia faces and appeals with great emotion and urgency for the United States to take the lead, like it always has, and come to Liberia's assistance in this urgent time of crisis. While she does not criticize the US Administration to her Congressional friends, she says that "the assistance so far by the US is insufficient. We need a large-scale mobilization. Now."

Some members reach out to the White House. Others, like Senators Leahy and Coons, make public statements. But even so, it is difficult breaking through during a highly scripted White House Summit, and on the edge of a month-long Congressional recess.

Our other self-assigned mission is to reach out to the private sector, those operating in the countries impacted by Ebola. If the disease cannot be controlled, their businesses could be destroyed, and the full capital investment lost. There is already information-sharing going on between companies in the mining sector. But how can we elevate an insular, single-industry focus and create a more integrated and global response?

While the rest of the Summit participants celebrate the growing business ties between Africa and the US, we call a meeting at the Lafayette Square Sofitel Hotel, chaired by Ambassador Malac. Half a dozen corporate members and representatives of the government of Liberia and NGOs are present. In a spirited discussion, the group suggests a number of action-steps. Business leaders will advocate, write letters, go to the media, and make cash donations to the NGOs. All worthwhile, but nothing that will have a direct and immediate impact. Then we switch gears and ask the question, What can we do, materially, now, to get others to come help? How can we jump-start the lagging global response? And then we land on the obvious. Half the battle in any disaster mobilization is logistics. The business community can offer its established and trusted supply chains—vehicles, drivers, living facilities, offices, generators, earthmoving equipment, catering, water purification, and trained staff. The companies have the ability to alleviate critical shortages of staff and capacity, including speeding up the construction of isolation and treatment centers that will be essential to containing the disease.

"With our collective footprint in the three most affected countries," Joe Matthews of ArcelorMittal later tells AllAfrica.com, "we have the wherewithal to provide logistical support to the various groups willing to mobilize personnel to these countries. Our companies can provide these medical teams and front-line health workers with transportation, drivers, decent accommodations, catering, laundry, as well as trained workers who can support this effort with administrative support. This will be an unprecedented private response to a global emergency—providing real support to those willing to risk their lives to help the people of Liberia, Sierra Leone and Guinea."

From that meeting and the efforts of the mining companies in the region there emerges the Ebola Private Sector Mobilization Group (EPS-MG), which grows to include several hundred corporate, NGO and public-sector members working together, across borders, to ensure that resources are maximized, and more important, that best practices in disease prevention are shared and adopted by institutions throughout the region.

These early August interventions with Congress and the business community matter a great deal. But the results are incremental actions, not the military-like mobilization of resources and personnel that we need. We have to find a way to bend the curve of the infection rate. It is climbing relentlessly. On August 17, MSF's Operations Director Brice de le Vigne tells the *Financial Times*, "We are completely amazed by the lack of willingness and professionalism and coordination to tackle this epidemic. We have been screaming for months."

On August 20 Tami Hultman of AllAfrica.com, one of the more aggressive and committed journalists pursuing the Ebola story, writes:

The World Health Organization this month is launching a U.S. $100 million disaster plan, after exhausting previous contributions of $7 million. The U.S. Centers for Disease Control (CDC) has sent 19 people to work in Liberia, and Public Affairs Director Barbara Reynolds says at least 60 CDC people are in Liberia, Guinea and Sierra Leone, plus Nigeria. Nobody who has been working on the Ebola crisis in Guinea, Sierra Leone or Liberia thinks that is close to what is needed.

Contrast that with the world response to the 2010 Haitian earthquake. Over $3.5 billion was donated by governments, organizations and individuals. Within 24 hours, the small nation of Israel had equipped a plane with emergency medical supplies, and 40 doctors and 20 nurses and 20 medics were able to set up a field hospital on arrival—including a patient identification system and electronic medical records. More than 300 CDC staff went to Haiti to assist in the recovery, including battling the ensuing cholera epidemic. In much of North America, Latin America and Europe, commercial businesses put out collection boxes for relief donations. Individuals responded massively.

Nothing like that is in place for West Africa.

In early September, Ellen and her team in Liberia are seeing little impact on the ground. They are feeling the futility of the incremental approach to fighting the disease. She decides that she needs to make a plea for help directly to world leaders, including President Obama. It will be personal and it will be desperate, a sounding of the alarm. Says Ellen, "I need to shock the consciousness of the world."

The first letter goes to President Obama. She writes:

I am being honest with you when I say that at this rate, we will never break the transmission chain and the virus will overwhelm us."

Mr. President, Liberia's peace and significant economic gains over the last 10 years have come at a great cost. Throughout this process, the United States has been a steadfast friend and partner. As impressive as our gains have been, they remain fragile and this outbreak now threatens to undermine those gains and reverse our progress. In view of this, I am directly appealing to you and the American people for the following:

A) That the US government sets up and operates at least one Ebola Treatment Unit (ETU) in Monrovia. Mr. President, at the current rate of infection, only governments like yours have the resources and assets to deploy at the pace required to arrest the spread. Branches of your military and civilian institutions already have the expertise in dealing with biohazard, infectious disease and chemical agents. They already understand appropriate infection control protocols and we saw these assets deployed in Aceh after the tsunami and in Haiti after the earthquake. It is in appreciation of the difference in kind of this disaster that we are requesting assistance from units with expertise in managing biohazards.

B) That the U.S. government assists in restoring regular basic and secondary health services in at least 10 non-Ebola hospitals. We have been told by healthcare workers on the frontline that only 80 percent of patients presenting symptoms at ETUs are infected with the virus. The other 20 percent needs to be treated at non-Ebola health facilities. However, we need appropriate infection control protocols and testing facilities to protect healthcare workers and non-Ebola patients in these facilities. Currently, in Monrovia there are 8 hospitals, ranging from 50 to 418 beds. Across the rest of the country we need to reopen at least one large public health facility to prevent deaths from treatable diseases and prevent maternal and infant mortality.

"Let's not wait for the letter to be delivered through official channels," says Gyude Moore, Ellen's dynamic deputy chief of staff, a graduate of Georgetown University's School of Foreign Service and recruited from the Liberian diaspora. I spent countless hours with Gyude during the unsettled period of the 2011 elections. Late at night, as we pondered life's choices in the shared company of Shirley Brownell, the director of communications, and Seward Cooper, the legal advisor to the president, if we came across a good idea, we would label it a "Club Beer Moment" after the local brew kept stocked in the office fridge.

"We don't have time for the State Department to transmit the letter through the chain of command," says Gyude, "then pass it on to some staffer at the National Security Council. We can't just sit around while more people die."

"Right," I agree. "We know what to do."

As soon as we confirm that Ambassador Malac has received the PDF from the office of the president, we are off. The letter is sent, via Liberia's ambassador to the US, Jeremias Sunlunteh, to each of the members of Congress whom President Sirleaf called in early August. Then another round of phone calls is organized through Phemie and Chris so Ellen can follow up personally. Within two days, members of the House and Senate go to the floor to deliver statements demanding US and global action. Gyude rushes Ellen's letter to Barack Obama to *New York Times* reporter Helene Cooper as an exclusive. Cooper, an American of Liberian descent, provides passionate reporting throughout the Ebola epidemic. She and her colleagues would eventually win a Pulitzer Prize in journalism for that coverage. On September 12 significant quotes from Ellen's letter are published on the front page of the *New York Times* and go viral on platforms around the world. *Liberian President Pleads With Obama for Assistance in Combating Ebola*. This was big. We had elevated Ellen's shout to the highest decibel in the American media.

Now we are getting somewhere. Next comes a visit to the region by Tom Friedan, director the US Center for Disease Control. His personal assessment of the public health danger results in the CDC's prediction that the infection rate, left on its current trajectory, could produce as many as 1.4 million Ebola cases by January 2015. That frightening scenario begins to get some serious attention from the US and global communities. We are about to get what we pleaded for, a worldwide emergency mobilization, just like when countries band together to provide relief after a natural disaster with mass casualties—as they should have done months earlier for the Ebola crisis.

♦

Just as advocacy efforts start to yield measurable results, Ebola crosses the Atlantic by way of a 45-year old Liberian national, Thomas Eric Duncan. He disembarks from an airplane at Dallas/Fort Worth International Airport. Two days after his arrival, experiencing a 103-degree fever, Duncan asks his girlfriend to drive him to the Texas Health Presbyterian Hospital Emergency Room. He is misdiagnosed with a possible stomach virus. When Duncan returns to the ER two days later, his condition is properly diagnosed—Ebola. But it is too late to save Duncan. He dies, in spite of the spirited intervention by the critical care team at the hospital. Two young women caregivers are infected. Panic spreads in Dallas and then briskly across the entire United States as a worried and uninformed public fears a possible pandemic that could overwhelm the most sophisticated healthcare delivery system in the world. Even the most liberal-minded people are heard voicing the opinion to ban Africans from entering the country. Two weeks later, Dr. Craig Spencer returns from Guinea-Conakry through JFK Airport in New York. He takes ill and is likewise diagnosed with Ebola, but only after having already taken a subway to a bar outside of Manhattan. Panic turns into frenzy.

With just 35 days to go before the Congressional elections of 2014 and the Senate up for grabs for the first time in years, Ebola becomes the September Surprise, and our newly formed EPSMG, a loose, voluntary coalition of member companies, is thrust onto the political frontlines to challenge some Republican members of Congress on their proposal to bar Liberians, Sierra Leoneans and Guineans from traveling to the US. All other business organizations go silent, including the US Chamber of Commerce and the National Manufacturers Association. It is too politically hot.

On October 18, representing the US Secretariat for the EPSMG, I tell *The Hill* newspaper, "There's a lot of emotion and fear, and that will drive the political conversation, but the solution lawmakers are putting on the table is contrary to logic and science." Another EPSMG member in London tells Bloomberg that same week, "We should be isolating

Ebola, not these nations." President Obama also weighs in. "We can't just cut ourselves off from West Africa, where this disease is raging. Trying to seal off an entire region of the world, if that were even possible, could actually make the situation worse" by causing people to evade screening.

After the presidential directive, a compromise is reached. The US Center for Disease Control sets up a complex screening process at major US airports to identify, then track and monitor any traveler from the region throughout the 21-day incubation period. This "pull aside and self-reporting" mechanism creates delays for all travelers from the region, but it does not obstruct the deployment of a healthcare force. An unintended consequence of the Ebola screening, though, is the further stigmatization of people from the region. On the US political front, the Republicans win control of the Senate.

◆

With the disease raging, a global coalition is finally formed, with the US agreeing to lead in Liberia. The UK assumes the same for Sierra Leone, and the French take the helm in Guinea. The UN forms the United Nations Emergency Ebola Response (UNMEER). President Obama announces that he will deploy the 101st Airborne to Liberia, a bold and politically courageous move, given the election year politics. But that is nothing compared to the bravery of the men and women on the ground, Liberian and international, who risk their lives to save the lives of others. There are the burial boys, shunned by their communities, who nevertheless continue their grim, essential work. There are the workers at the crematorium fending off protestors and operating the site even though cremation violates Liberian cultural practices. There is the government official, Holy Koran in hand, who visits every Imam in the country to persuade them that Islam does allow for a different way of caring for the sick and the dead in times of plague and contagion. There are the midwives who craft makeshift gloves patched together with duct tape, delivering babies from mothers who are bleeding heavily in labor even when it is not known if the mothers are infected. There is Brussels Airlines, its management and crew, and Royal Air Moroc, the two airlines that remain operational throughout the epidemic to keep the air bridge open for first responders and humanitarian workers.

There is even the single US senator who has the courage to travel to the region and personally witness conditions on the ground, Chris Coons (D-DE), the Ranking Democrat on the Africa Subcommittee of the Senate Foreign Relations Committee. There are the businesses that stay and keep their essential operations going, care for their workers, the workers' families and their communities. There are the journalists who fearlessly cover the story of the disease and whose detailed field reporting will not let the world turn away from the emergency. The US military, whose very presence alongside the Armed Force of Liberia (AFL) lifts the spirit of an entire nation, sends a signal that the country has not been abandoned. They put in place, with precision and efficiency, a logistical bridge and supply chain that is essential in getting help to those who need it, even in the interior of the country.

Then there is Ellen, steadfast and in command. For eight months she refuses to leave the country, with the exception of one regional summit, until the very last Ebola patient is ready to leave the ETU. She presides over the government response in Monrovia, ensuring there is coordination of all national and international responders. She travels to the communities most devastated by the disease to press for the cooperation of religious, tribal, and youth leaders, urging them to self-police and ensure all health and safety protocols are observed. She seeks out every means of media and communication, uses every contact she has, to beg, plead, shame, argue and demand that the world come to Liberia's aid.

◆

On May 4, 2015, barely seven months after the US Center for Disease Control made its frightening prediction, the World Health Organization declares Liberia Ebola-free. It is a stunning accomplishment. The entire world seems to breathe a sigh of relief. When one month later five additional cases are identified in the country, healthcare workers stomp them out with the protocols that have been learned, tested and perfected during the crisis. Sierra Leone and Guinea, meanwhile, continue to struggle to contain a greatly weakened but still persistent Ebola outbreak.

Finally, in January of 2016, the entire sub-region is declared Ebola-free, after more than 12,000 people die of the disease, with Liberia losing more than 4,800 of its citizens. Much of the world does not realize how hard this was to achieve, nor how frightfully close we were to a full-blown global epidemic.

There were many lessons learned in combating Ebola and many mistakes made. The failure to recognize immediately the seriousness of the disease was one. Failing to understand the latent distrust of government within the Liberian communities was another. It took time to dispel people's disbelief about the lethal nature of the illness and to embrace the community's essential role in responding to the crisis. The international response came late, weighed down by denial and bureaucratic lethargy.

"Never again" is now the mantra. But the threat of Ebola returning to the region remains real. So does the possibility that another viral contagion will emerge with the potential to disrupt our global health security. The fear I heard in Ellen's voice that August day will never leave me. It is my own constant reminder.

In the fight against Ebola, the world saw the Ellen that I have always known. The fighter, the woman, the mom who will not give up, even when so much is against her. The Ellen who is humble enough to draw lessons from her failures and gain strength doing so. A listener, a leader who knows she does not have all the answers. Relentless when necessary, and single-minded in her pursuits. Throughout her life, Ellen Johnson Sirleaf has been utterly consistent. It has always been the well-being of the Liberian people that she desired most, their future and promise that she sought to advance.

It was this Ellen who found me in 1996 at a low point in my life. She believed in me when I doubted almost everything about myself. She gave me the great gift of her friendship and wisdom. I have often reflected on how grateful I am that I chose Ellen to follow and believe in. But sometimes I wonder whether, after all, it is really Ellen who chose me.

Monrovia Liberia, February 2015

AFTERWORD

Africa and the world has changed a lot since I met Ellen in July of 1996. While there are a handful of leaders who still hang on to power in Africa, and civil conflict persists in places like South Sudan and the Great Lakes Region, for the most part Sub-Saharan Africa is moving toward peace and improved governance. A large middle-class with real purchasing power is emerging and excelling. The scourge of government corruption, which two decades ago was considered institutionalized and woven into the fabric of African life, is now being unknotted and replaced with sustainable economic practice. A young population is rising up to challenge leaders who steal and enrich themselves. Technology and digital innovation have empowered the individual, creating greater mobility of commerce, strengthening community-based structures and allowing the free flow of ideas. Africa is fast becoming an incubator for new ideas. A new generation of entrepreneurs is creating rapidly growing consumer markets.

Ellen has been part of this great transition. But now Liberia is at a crossroads. In 2016 the United Nations Mission in Liberia (UNMIL) departs. It has kept the peace for 13 years. Internal and external security will be the task of Liberia's National Police and its armed forces. This may pose a challenge, given the limited resources of the government, and it will be a test of discipline for a young force. In October 2017 the country will hold its third national elections since the establishment of peace, and for the first time, Ellen Johnson Sirleaf will not be on the ballot. At stake are the democratic and economic institutions that she and her government have built. I remember Ellen's statement to me that one of the greatest challenges the country would face is its "political immaturity."

But now after Ebola, after witnessing the social cohesion and resiliency in the Liberian communities, their readiness to fight to defend themselves and their families, and to safeguard their future, I am convinced that the Liberian people will keep their politicians in check. They will demand the best of their leaders.

Where Ellen will be in Liberia's next phase of development remains to be seen. She speaks of taking a rest, but those of us who know her well, know that rest for Ellen usually does not last more than a few days. "There is still so much to do!" is Ellen's signature refrain. She is referring to Liberia, and to Africa, but also to women throughout the developing world. Whatever role she takes next, she will serve as a model of political leadership. We all need leaders who show courage, serve with conviction and integrity, appreciate that power must be wielded with wisdom and moderation, and ultimately know when to make way for the next generation. Ellen's peaceful transition from public office will set the example—for Africa and for the world.

Working with Ellen has taught me to follow my heart and not to fear being misunderstood. I have come to see that certainty is a luxury and destiny a journey that reveals itself with time. It is easy to stray off course, to doubt and lose faith, to see compromise as surrender, to feel judged, isolated and even abandoned. But there is always something to hold on to, the belief that things will get better. I have come to appreciate that we need people to guide us, those we admire and those we believe in—the heroes that we choose.

Ellen and Riva in November 2007 at the White House on day President George W. Bush awards President Johnson Sirleaf with Presidential Medal of Freedom.

INDEX

President Ellen Johnson Sirleaf holding Financial Times Liberia report, December 9, 2011, on day before Nobel Peace Laureate Award, Oslo.

ACKNOWLEDGMENTS

To so many people, I express my heartfelt thanks.

First, my family. To my husband Jeff who never second-guessed my life's choices, remained supportive of my missions even when he had his doubts, and posed the same simple questions each time: "Where and when do I pick you up?" To my children, Kylie and Andrew, who put up with their show-and-tell Mom and all that went with it; I am in awe of the young adults they have become. To my sister Kim and my cousin Glen who helped me research the life of my grandmother, Oma: Thank you for preserving our family archives. To my aunt Ellie, the family's matriarch and greatest archive.

To my publisher-on-a-mission, David Applefield of Kiwai Media, and to John Strand, editor and playwright-in-residence at Arena Stage in Washington, DC. David and John brought my book to life. Without them, my writing would have remained a collection of random pages, stacked under my bed, never to be shared. To Mayanne Wright for proofreading the pages. To my agent Paul Fedorko, who committed to represent me even when he wasn't sure in which direction my story would go. Paul said to me, "What I am certain of is that few people have walked in your shoes. But my question remains, who the hell would want to?"

To all the people who believed in my story before there was one really worth telling. To Elise D'Hane and Stacey Donovan who helped me catalog my early missions and stories more than a decade ago and taught me how to write with consequence. To my Liberian reviewing team that included Abdoulaye "Duke" Dukulé, Phemie Brewer and Conmany Wesseh. To Elizabeth Sheehy for her priceless proofreading.

To my two former interns, Steven Brown, who has been pressing me to write a book for the past fifteen years and introduced me to everyone and anyone to help get it done; and in memory of David Miller, my very first intern at Black, Manafort, Stone & Kelly, who was the only person in the firm who pushed the limits of corporate constraints more than I did. It was David who first introduced me to Ellen.

To Steve Cashin, Dr. Deborah Harding and Billy Register, Ellen's Swat Team, her friends who gave their all to help Ellen succeed. With a special thanks to Steve, who has been a friend and supporter for almost two decades.

To my longtime client and friend Brad Horwitz. It was his commercial battles that sharpened my skills so I could fight the good fight for Ellen.

To my professional mentors and dear friends Peter Kelly and Sean Cleary whose counsel has guided me personally and professionally for nearly 30 years. Both have helped me navigate a challenging world and profession with integrity and heart.

To my many friends and colleagues in and outside of Washington, D.C. who taught me about the world, Africa, and the meaning of friendship. They include Dr. Raymond Gilpin, Theresa Whelan, Pam Fields Miner, Peter Henderson, April Sabo and family, the Sheehy family, Lisa Lebowtiz and family, Linda and Sam Dark, the memory of Nell Haymaker, Natalie San Pedro, John Donaldson, Peter Tichansky, Bob Perry, Mark Clack, Reed Kramer, Tami Hultman and Eric Chinje. Special thanks to Todd Moss, who was insistent that I write this book.

Special thanks also to Chris Beatty, KRL's Managing Director, for his dedication to our Liberian friends, and our fearless team at KRL International, Afi Akolly, Laura Brunts and Danielle Johnson, and our great alumni.

I thank the US government officials who advocated for Liberia even when there were so many competing foreign policy objectives. Thanks to the staff of the members of Congress, some of whom are mentioned in this book, who are the unsung heroes in Liberia's saga, and who made great contributions to Liberia's post-conflict success.

I thank my fellow congregants at Temple Rodef Shalom in Falls Church, Virginia, and our clergy with whom I traveled in November 2014 to Berlin, Auschwitz and Birkenau. It is one thing to be taught, another to be told, and a completely different experience to see for yourself.

To all of my Liberian friends, too many to name here, who made me a part of their extended families and a partner in the country's struggle and emergence from conflict. And to Amara Konneh, my partner-on-the-ground during the 2005 elections, who would go on to be Liberia's Minister of Planning and Finance Minister.

And finally, my gratitude to Ellen Johnson Sirleaf, whose friendship I hold dear as one of the great gifts of my life, and whose courageous achievements continue to serve as an inspiration for a rising Africa and a new generation of women and girls. I hope this book gives her some sense of the meaning she has brought to my life and to all the lives she has touched.

—RIVA